True Rebellion

VOLUME 2
The Way of the Heart

The Way of the Heart

Copyright © 2025 by Vishrant. All rights reserved.

No part of this book may be reproduced, stored in a retrieval system, or transmitted in any form or by any means, including electronic, mechanical, photocopying, recording, or otherwise, or translated into any language, without prior written permission from the author and publisher, except for brief quotations used in reviews or articles.

True Rebellion Vol. 2
The Way of the Heart
ISBN:
978-1-7638511-6-0 - ebook
978-1-7638511-7-7 - paperback
The Vishrant Buddhist Society

Disclaimer

This book is intended for educational and informational purposes only. The insights and teachings shared within this book reflect the personal experiences and understandings of Vishrant and are not intended as professional advice. The content of this book should not be used as a substitute for medical, psychological, legal, or financial advice. Readers are encouraged to use their discernment and seek professional guidance where necessary.

The author and publisher make no representations or warranties regarding the completeness, accuracy, or applicability of the teachings presented. The journey of self-inquiry and spiritual awakening is deeply personal, and each individual is responsible for their own path and experiences.

Contents

Overview 5
Introduction 7

CHAPTER ONE
The Way of the Heart 9

CHAPTER TWO
Finding Truth in the Era of New Age Spirituality 31

CHAPTER THREE
How to Deal with Uncertainty 57

CHAPTER FOUR
How to Use Relationships for Higher Consciousness 85

CHAPTER FIVE
Overcoming Suffering 105

CHAPTER SIX
The Only Chance Humanity Has to Survive 133

CHAPTER SEVEN
The Peace in Becoming No One 155

CHAPTER EIGHT
The Recipe for Success in Spirituality 179

CHAPTER NINE
What Are Energy-Clearing Practices? 211

CHAPTER TEN
What Are the Obstacles to Happiness? 237

About Vishrant 263

Overview

True Rebellion is a four-part series delving deeply into the most crucial challenges faced by today's seekers. Vishrant's teachings are focused on seekers living and working in the marketplace, just as he did in his years-long journey towards Enlightenment.

Each volume of the True Rebellion series provides critical insight into the private workings of Vishrant's Mystic Heart Mystery School located in the hills of Perth near the historic Araluen Estate. Seekers from around the world attend in person and online in what may be the only Mystery School personally run by an enlightened master. Vishrant credits his years in Osho's Mystery School in Oregon and Pune for his own preparation for Enlightenment.

Vishrant sees that teachers who claim "there is nothing to do" are selling seekers short. He says seekers deserve the truth full strength and to understand that the obstacles that are in the way of Enlightenment must be undone if the seeker is to reach the ultimate. Although those who seek awakening must ultimately surrender themselves in the achievement, Vishrant's teachings are focused on helping ardent students of higher consciousness ready themselves for that awakening to occur.

The True Rebellion series was produced with this expressed purpose in mind: to highlight and deeply examine the key challenges and obstacles seekers face as hindrances to Enlightenment. The four-book series explores topics including family and work commitments, self-doubt, failure patterns, inherited programming, and the role of the mind and the need for scepticism, openness, present-moment awareness and trust on the path to higher consciousness and Enlightenment.

Vishrant's dialogues with students also provide numerous real-world examples from the master's own journey towards Enlightenment after he found himself as Truth in 1999 following many years of totality as a seeker. The exchanges recorded in the True Rebellion series contain Vishrant's trademark wit and humour, as well as the cutting insights and ruthless honesty he says every seeker must also develop for themselves.

Introduction

Imagine a world where there was no selfishness and no self-obsession. We would have such a beautiful place, but we don't. We live in the world that we live in, and it's the way it is, but we as individuals can choose the way we live in this world, and for me the Way of the Heart is the best way to live because it is so beautiful.

It does mean that at some point you need to put yourself aside, because the Way of the Heart requires a certain absence of you in the picture, mostly because you've been programmed simply to survive, and in a lot of ways that doesn't involve putting yourself aside for others or putting yourself aside for the planet or taking care, and the Way of the Heart is really a caring role – caring about the impression you make on this world.

Are you a caretaker here? Are you taking care of the planet? Are you taking care of the people on this planet? Are you taking care of the plants and the animals on this planet or are you just living here as someone who uses the planet?

When we look at the Way of the Heart, it is really a caretaking role: to be kind, to be generous, caring, and I think most religions teach this. Somewhere in their dogma, there is some of this teaching, but I like to remove all of the dogma, all of the belief systems, and just stay with a way of life that supports Heart, what I call the Beauty Way. And that's up to you as an individual. It's not up to anyone else.

Nobody can do it for you. Nobody can even help you in it. It's your attitude and what you do in the world that brings that about. It's not easy, because we're designed to survive, and part of putting yourself aside is putting survival aside, putting righteousness aside, allowing yourself to be vulnerable and open and sometimes helpless instead of defended and sharp. It is allowing yourself to be an ear for others, instead of a broadcasting system.

This is a whole way of life. This isn't something you do at night time or after work or on weekends. This is how you are every moment. It's a way of living. It's the Way of the Heart.

This is your opportunity to rise above the animal level, because when we serve Heart, we raise ourselves above the animal level. We raise ourselves above survival and we live a noble life, which tends to be a life of service and devotion to others.

And it's absolutely up to you. No one will ever make you. No one will probably even try to persuade you. You have to choose it for yourself.

CHAPTER ONE

The Way of the Heart

V: *dialog from Vishrant*
S: *dialog from student*
~ *separate dialogues from different speakers*

V: Welcome to satsang.

About 34 years ago, I had this realisation that I had wasted 33 years of my life in service of myself and in service of being successful in the material world. And I'm not saying there's anything wrong with that, but for me, it cost me my Heart.

As a businessman, I'd turned myself into a war machine and I was pretty good at it, but 34 years ago, I had an awakening of the Heart and it changed my life completely. I could not see any point in making money for the sake of making money anymore. I felt that it was repetitious, and for me, it was relatively easy.

So after having this awakening, which disappeared, I realised there was something very, very valuable here for human beings, and that was the Heart or unconditional love. It didn't take too long, from that point. It took about nine months before I walked into my companies and gave them to my staff as a gift. I cared about my staff. They'd been with me for 10 years or more and I didn't want to see the company sold and them possibly get sacked or whatever could have happened to them, so I gave my staff everything, including the office furniture. So 35 of them were reasonably happy and I walked out broke.

I had realised that as long as I was in business as a publisher, which is a very hectic business, I was too closed, too defended, too protected to perceive love. I had come to an understanding that love was possible for human beings – unconditional love – but only under certain conditions. And those conditions were openness, vulnerability and being undefended.

So we hear about people wearing their hearts on their sleeves. Well yes, you have to be that open – and the problem with that, of course, is that if you are that open, the world will hurt you. The world is pretty rough. People betray you. They let you down. They say things. They steal. All sorts of things happen that don't go the way you would like, and quite often we close to defend ourselves. In so doing, we cut ourselves off from the perception of love, and love is really the true jewel of consciousness.

After about four years of wandering around Australia barefoot as a bum, I found my Heart. Existence broke me. I surrendered enough of my defence systems – enough of my resistance to life – to perceive love regularly. I had developed a pattern of undoing defence systems and being open, and as time went by, more and more love was perceived.

It's kind of like around that point that I realised there's nothing else worth doing here. I could never really find a true purpose for life or a meaningful life, even though I had been looking since I was a young teenager. But if I'm going to be here, what I decided was, I might as well love. And when love affects the mind, you just want to take care of everything and everyone – that's how beautiful it is – the good, the bad, and the ugly, your enemies and your friends. Love is most magnificent, but there's a price for it. It is your openness. It is your undefendedness. It is your non-resistance to life and your acceptance of life as it is.

And that, for a lot of us, especially for me, was very difficult. I had gone to a private school where I was taught how to win at any cost, and I took that into my 20s into business as a war machine. I had to dismantle the war machine. I had to take down all of its defence systems. I had to start to walk through the world open, even while being attacked, because I felt that love was more important than anything. I'm not really talking about personal love here. Not "I love you" or "I love my partner" or "I love my children". I love everybody and everything. And this is possible if you're willing to be open, if you're willing to experience the discomfort of being open, because it is uncomfortable to be open, to be around the roughness of the world we live in. It is hard and it takes courage. So people get into higher consciousness and they start looking for Enlightenment.

But while you're looking, you've still got to be here, and as far as I'm concerned, the only way to be here that's worthwhile is the Way of the Heart. This path is the path of non-resistance. People say, "Well, if I'm non-resistant, I'll be ineffective in the world; if I'm open, I'll be ineffective in the world". Not true. We can do everything from openness. We just think we can't. We can be very effective, but from a place that will support Heart rather than from a place that just supports survival.

So sometimes I talk about Enlightenment, but towards Enlightenment there's a way to live in this place, a beautiful way to live in this place, and this is the Way of the Heart. It's up to you as to whether you do or you don't. No one will ever make you. No one will ever make you take your defences down. You have to voluntarily do it yourself, and I'd never, ever tell anyone that it was easy because it's not. Changing any default pattern in the mind is difficult. It takes a fair bit of practice over a fair bit of time, but what else have you got to do? How beautiful is your life? Because when you serve Heart, it may be uncomfortable, but it's beautiful.

Any questions, any statements, any challenges to this teaching this evening?

S: Hello. Is there an element of grace involved in going for Enlightenment?

V: That's a funny word: grace. When a spiritual teacher says grace, what they're really saying is they don't know. Is there an element of grace? It could be an element of karma – whatever we put into life, we get back – but I don't really understand grace. It seems like a word to cover "I don't know". If you open up and you become vulnerable, you'll perceive love, but that's up to you. No one can make you. People say,

"Well, I love my wife or I love my husband, I love my kids". How about loving everybody and not being able to help it? That's the possibility. Always be open. See defensiveness as in the way.

Tosh, can you get reports for me please?
S: Yes. Bodhi, your report.
S: Yes. I was wondering, did it take you a long time to remove your defence systems?
V: Piece by piece, it was taken down. Sometimes you take down a piece, you'll undo it all and you'll find it there the next day or the next moment, but I was quite determined. I'd got to a point where I realised that you can't actually be happy by getting things. I was successful as a young man. I got everything. Doesn't make you happy. People think "Well, if I get the house, if I get the wife, if I get the good car, if I have a good job, if I get paid a lot of money, I'll be happy". No. That's a lie. If you find Heart, you can be happy. Loving things is beautiful. They say the Way of the Heart is the Noble Path. I would tend to agree. You take care of even your enemies because you love them.

Yes?
S: You were mentioning about unconditional love. I've experienced that ... the time in my life through my most vulnerable times.
V: Yes.
S: But I also experienced terror.
V: Yes.
S: It was terrifying going through that time, but in return I had amazing experiences.
V: Yes.

S: And the gentlemen who explained about Heart opening ... the gentlemen who asked about what it feels like, what I felt was beyond words. It's an experience of love that – I'm a bit beyond words – that brings you to tears of joy. A feeling that you will never usually experience ever in your life, but it comes and it goes and it comes and it goes and it only comes when you surrender.

V: Yes, and the reason you can't describe it is because we don't have any reference points in the ego to describe it. And it does come and go and did come and go until I found a way to lay everything down and keep it down. So every time I found myself in resistance to anything, I undid whatever belief system was supporting that resistance so it wouldn't happen again, because I was determined to serve Heart rather than serve survival. And it felt like I'd been skinned alive when I first started doing it, walking around with humans without armour on.

S: Scary.

V: Yeah. But you know, we get used to it. It becomes ordinary. It's extraordinary in the beginning because it's unusual, but after a while it becomes ordinary. You've just got to be a little careful that you don't tell everyone you love them, especially the Coles checkout girls. They just don't appreciate it. And I didn't think it was possible. I just had to have a go at it.

If you really examine your life, you can't find a purpose or a meaning for it. And I've heard every purpose and every meaning that everyone's thought of. When I really got honest with myself, I couldn't find a purpose. I thought, "Well, I have to be here. What should I do if I'm here?" And it had to be love. So I became a servant of love. A servant of the Heart, really. And the deal that I found that worked best was "everything for Heart and nothing for me". That also happens to be the same deal for Enlightenment: everything for Truth and nothing for me.

V: James, would you like to give a report?

S: Lovely to be back. I missed you.

V: Good to see you, James.

S: Excellent to see you. Excellent to see you. I missed you.

V: Would you like to give a report?

S: What is happening for me is that during the day I am experiencing a lot of spaciousness and the feeling of being pulled into Beingness, but I can't seem to let go in those moments.

V: So what actually came up for me is that I had to be willing to die because all of our defence systems are about survival, and as long as we're trying to survive, we're defended. And if we really look at being undefended, it's a death.

And ultimately, when those defences arise and you're standing at the edge of survival and annihilation, what do you do?

I played a game called zero. Zero was when I was flatlined, when I was wide open. Anything above zero was resistance of some kind, and anytime I went above zero, my mind would notice the rise and I'd have a look and see what was it that's taking me above zero. What is it that I'm resisting and what belief systems are attached to that resistance? Because usually there are belief systems attached to it. Then I'd undo the belief system. I'd discredit it because I didn't want to hold on to anything that kept me above zero, and I played the game of zero for 10 years. Nobody knew I was playing it. It was my game, but if you upset me and I went above zero, I'd be looking. I'd be more interested in why I was above zero than in being right with you. So it became a game for me, a spiritual game of "let's stay at zero". And at zero, I could feel love. Sometimes it wasn't strong, but it was always there. And sometimes it was overwhelming, it was so beautiful.

But really, it was a death. Ultimately, it was unconditional surrender, which is a death, and that's hard, because we can't actually do unconditional surrender. We can only do acceptance. Acceptance is still a doing, that with the practise of acceptance, we get to unconditional surrender. We accept everything as it is without resistance. It's like walking through the world as a dead man. You're so alive, but you're not resisting life. You see everything because you're settled back. You're not engaged. You have detachment and you feel love. You perceive love. You see the suffering in the world and there's a lot of it. And this drives you to wanting to take care.

There's another game I play. The game is pretty simple. Everyone I meet, how can I help them? How can I lift them in some way? Whether it's humour or a hello or money or whatever, how can I help you? It's another game. It's a game that helps Heart. When we look at it, if there was more love on this planet, we wouldn't have global warming, we wouldn't have people starving, we wouldn't have wars, we wouldn't have terrorism because love takes care, has you taking care of everything and everyone. Unfortunately, I think there's a lack of love on this planet, and as a result, we're seeing what we're seeing. So you can't change the world, but you can change yourself, and it's up to us as individuals if we want to do something to change ourselves.

What's your name, sir?
S: It's Pete.
V: Hi Pete, good to have you here.
S: When you were on your walk around Australia, how did you support yourself?
V: I used to do odd jobs here and there. I used to go to soup kitchens. I was literally a bum. I knew how to make money. I knew how to get back into the world if I wanted to, but I didn't want to. I'd had enough. I'd seen enough. I'd been around the block enough times to realise that I did not want to do that anymore, that there was something better here. But I didn't really know how to get it because I was too closed. I was like a Sherman tank and I had to undo all of the armour and take it off. So I stayed with people. Sometimes if I was in a town, I'd find a party to go to and someone would take me home. It was so interesting to go from my life, which was driving a Rolls Royce, to being an absolute bum and relying on the goodwill of other people to take care of me. It taught me humility.

S: Were you out of touch with your family during this time?

V: Well, that's why I eventually came back, to take care of people back in Perth. I ended up in Byron Bay for a while, not long, but a while, and I eventually came back here to take care of a family that had left me. When I came back, I went back to school and trained as a naturopath and a psychotherapist to have the skills to actually help people. As a businessman, that's all I was good at: being a businessman. As a naturopath and psychotherapist, I put myself through school and my partner through school. I eventually married her. We had two children and we homeschooled those children. I worked from a clinic at the front of the house that I lived in. It was just a rented house because I wasn't wealthy anymore, but I really loved people. I loved what I did. I loved my children. I loved my wife. I loved my clients. I loved my neighbours. I just loved and it was beautiful. I had the same problems like everybody else. Things go wrong, but I'd learnt not to resist life. I'd learnt to accept it, and when you don't resist life, you don't suffer. We only really suffer when we resist life. Bad things happen. It can be painful, it can be uncomfortable, but it's only when we resist that we suffer. So I stopped suffering, which is nice. How conscious do you want to be? As you become more and more conscious there's a lot of things you don't want to be involved in anymore. Is there anything more?

S: No, thank you.

~

S: Good morning.
V: Good to see you here.
S: Hello, sir.
V: You're welcome here. I don't think I've seen you before. You've come to an unusual room.

~

V: It's good to see you, Rebecca.
S: Hello. Would it be at all possible to be outwardly violent while inwardly loving?
V: So if you're inwardly loving, you're wide open inside, you're not closed. You're not defended, but you could still be aggressive outside while being open. It's just that most of the time when we're aggressive, we close to protect ourselves from what might be coming back. An example of that is we might need to read the riot act to our kids because they're out of order. We can do that from a place of love and openness while still being quite aggressive in what we're saying outside, but I wouldn't call that violence. It's just being aggressive, because sometimes that's what's required if needs be. Can we do it, though, from a place of openness and love internally? Yes, we can.

Okay? I don't think it's possible to be violent outside if you're open, okay?
S: How do you accept violence in others?
V: I found it inside of myself and found a way to love it inside of myself. I think we have everything inside of us really, from my observation of my mind, and when I found it inside of myself and found a way to accept it and love it inside of myself, I didn't have a

problem after that, outside of myself, with that sort of person.

S: What about if that violence is being inflicted on me or my children?

V: I understand what you're saying to me. It doesn't mean I wouldn't move to action to stop that, but I'd love them while I was doing it. I couldn't help myself because I know that part inside of me and there but for the grace of God goes I. You don't know my history, but I had quite a violent upbringing and so I understand violence. Is there anything else?

S: Thank you.

~

S: Can you comment please on why I find it so difficult to be considered less important or not important sometimes in social situations?

V: Yes, you have to allow yourself to be "less-than". We're always trying to be "more-than". You have to allow yourself to be less-than, and that takes practice because we're so good at being more-than. You have to allow yourself to be seen as the loser, rather than the constant winner. You have to allow yourself to put yourself aside, when you know you're right. You have to become the servant instead of the master.

Practice. So what is it that you want to do? How is it that you don't want to be seen? Are you humble enough to be seen in any light, in any way, or are there some things that you couldn't allow yourself to be seen? So I went to all of the places that I didn't want to go and stayed there until there was nothing left. Higher consciousness, in a lot of ways, is a

great undoing. It's not about adding anything. That's personal growth. It's about undoing – undoing everything, reverse engineering everything, until you're wide, wide open. It's easy to be resistant. It's easy to be strong. It's not so easy to be open and vulnerable. It takes practice. If you're interested in the Heart, I don't know any other way. While we're being resistant and strong, we probably aren't perceiving love. We're too closed to it, too separate from it.
S: Yes.

~

S: Is chanting helpful?
V: It wasn't helpful for me, but it might be helpful for someone else. I didn't go that way, the chanting or the.... It is the bhakti path I chose, but I also chose the path of discipline: both paths. I didn't stay on one. I was a meditator, and I was into self-inquiry, and the practice of zero is also discipline. At the same time, I was into giving and taking care of. I was into the Way of the Heart. So both bhakti and the path of discipline, I think, is what serves us who live in the marketplace. I think if we're only going to do jnani, we might as well go to a monastery or a cave or an ashram, and that might work, but if we're in the marketplace, I think we need the bhakti and we need the discipline. Without the discipline, we don't learn to develop a mind that will support Truth. Without discipline, we don't self-inquire. Without discipline, we don't change. Without love, we don't end up falling in love with Truth. It is the love of Truth that brings you home. Does that answer that for you?

S: You said when you were walking around Australia looking for your Heart, you knew this was something better than what you were doing before, but did you experience it?

V: The memory, the memory of what unconditional love was – my mind had become very attracted to it, very addicted to it, because it couldn't see much point in continuing just making money for the sake of making money. It seemed like a waste of life. Whereas love is so beautiful. It was worthy. It was a worthy quest.

S: Did you experience frustration when you couldn't find Heart?

V: Yes, but I also saw frustration as resistance as another thing that was in the way of Heart so I dropped that too.

S: Is there ever a time to support anger in ourselves? I was listening to an audio book about anger and he was talking about using gratitude to overcome anger.

V: I tend to disagree. The only reason we can be angry is when we turn ourselves into a victim of circumstance, a situation, another human being, or ourselves. If we don't turn ourselves into a victim and start blaming, it's very difficult to be angry. If we remove the blame completely – refuse ever to be a victim – anger cannot arise, but that takes a lot of practice if you've been using anger – which is a defence system – for a long time. Anger stops us from feeling what's been touched, and it works, but unfortunately, it's a form of violence and it doesn't build bridges. It destroys them. So it's up to you. You're the one who creates your reality. You are the one who supports blame. You're the one who supports victim-orientated thinking. You do. So it's up to you. You're responsible. You can't get help from outside of you. It has to come from inside of you.

I think it's a Band-Aid. I don't think it works. There's nothing wrong with gratitude. But I think when we're dealing with anger, we need to be a little bit more precise. Anger was my problem as a teenager. I had to learn to deal with it. I learned that if I didn't support victim-orientated thinking, the anger didn't survive. It died. At some point, I realised that life is not good or bad, life is just what is. It's nothing to be a victim over.

It's great to have you here.

S: You said that if you can see parts of yourself that are dark, you can meet others with understanding?
V: If you own them and love them? Yes. If you own them, accept them and love them? Yes. If you shun them, reject them and abandon them? No. What you turn inside yourself into an enemy, you will find that you will see it the same way outside of yourself. When we love those parts inside of ourselves, we will feel compassion and empathy for those who haven't seen them yet who are operating them externally.

The judgments may be correct. You may see someone being violent and you may have a judgment, "that's not okay," but because you've seen it inside of yourself, you can hold that person in love, while maybe even stopping them from what they're doing.
S: Does practising the game of zero help?
V: Well, the methodology of zero creates equanimity. Yes: a mind that doesn't react to the world, but responds to the world.

S: I have a belief system that when I say sorry to somebody, they should display leniency or understanding.
V: You have a belief system that people should give you understanding when you apologise?
S: Yeah.
V: Ooh, that could get you into trouble, couldn't it? I definitely don't have that belief system. Matter of fact, I don't give apology a great deal of merit. It's too cheap.
S: Yeah, I feel like I got angry today. It felt like rejection.
V: If you don't have a belief system that you shouldn't be rejected, it's not a problem. Why shouldn't people reject you? You reject people. Anything else?

~

S: I noticed today I get caught in procrastination, like with my current break-up, and thoughts come up like, "Have I done the right thing?" Just wondering, could you give me some advice about what I'm doing and how to get through this?
V: If we look at why you're debating things in your mind, you're trying to avoid discomfort, you're trying to avoid pain. Once you become willing to actually feel the pain of loss, the mind doesn't need to actually try to escape by analysing and procrastinating any longer. The analysing, the procrastination, is a result of your mind trying to escape feeling something. And so it comes back to a willingness to feel the discomfort.
S: So the practice is to just feel everything that comes up?

V: Everything, without resistance, without diversion. My Heart goes out to you.

~

S: Noticed today I start opening up and experiencing something coming up in me and then I noticed that I start to close again, and then consciously trying to remain open.

V: Well, that's what the game of zero was for me: spotting that I'd closed a little bit and then opening up again and then working out why I'd closed, because if we don't have a look at why we close, even if we do open up, if the same trigger comes, we're likely to close again. And so the idea is to work out how to not close by undoing anything that's facilitating the closure, which is defensiveness.

S: Thank you.

~

S: They landed a probe on Mars last night.

V: How do you know? What if that wasn't real?

S: Could be fake.

V: What do we know is real?

S: What's happening right now.

V: That's it, that's it, and only what we can see and hear and feel right now. Everything else is a maybe.

S: Maybe NASA landed a probe on Mars last night. Thank you.

V: Hang on a second. Do we know that NASA's real? Have we been there? Are we there right now?

S: No.

V: The plot thickens. I think we have a NASA scientist online right now. Yes, we do. Susha works for NASA.

~

S: There's a part of me that feels like I'm not doing enough with my life when I see these things.
V: We have a million and one ways to make ourselves feel uncomfortable.
S: I've got this belief that being ordinary or average isn't okay.
V: Right. So being less-than would be very difficult.
S: Well, yes. This is what it brought up this morning.
V: Yeah, it's difficult to actually allow yourself to feel the ordinariness of yourself because we've all been programmed to compete. It's what school did to us. We've always been programmed to be better than someone else and then get a mark for it. It's sad, really, because it sets us against each other, and it really is against the Way of the Heart.

I've got this deal with winning. It's a really good deal. If I win, everyone has to win. Otherwise, I'm not interested in winning. You have to examine inside of yourself what it means to compete when other people are losing. And how does that make you feel that other people lose as a result of your winning? If you're in touch with your Heart, it'll hurt you. Anything else?
S: No. Thank you.

~

V: Hello.
S: Hi, Vish. A while ago you said that all you had to do was to touch the door handle to your office and step through, and the story of you would go and you'd be left with your client.

V: Yes

S: How did you start to bring this into your life completely?

V: So the story goes that when I had a naturopathic clinic and psychotherapy clinic at the front of my house, I'd do my family thing, and when I touched the door of my clinic to go in, the story of Vishrant would disappear completely. I'd be just there for the people on the other side of the door. And there came a point when I realised that was a very peaceful way to live. The story of Vishrant was not a peaceful story because it had a lot of drama in it, like everyone else's life. But I realised that I had enough control of my mind not to run the story of Vishrant when I went to my clinic. So then at some point, I decided to not run the story of Vishrant ever again.

S: Did that happen all of a sudden or was it gradual?

V: It was gradual. It was an epiphany that blew my mind because here I am dealing with clients, they've got their problems, but I don't have any because I didn't take any into the room. I was just there as a vehicle for them to facilitate what they needed, and this became evident that this was very peaceful without the story of Vishrant and his problems. Doesn't mean I didn't have problems in life. It just meant I didn't dwell on them.

S: I was told by a friend who used to be my manager that it's easier to leave "me" out of the workspace as much as possible, and I found it very peaceful.

V: Yeah, you obviously have the ability to. It's just, can you bring it into the rest of your life? Can you bring

that peace into the rest of your life which has been brought about by you not entertaining your drama? The moment we accept life as it is, all drama ceases.
S: Thank you.
V: Thank you.

~

S: I remember you talking about, if we practise openness, that we can change forever?
V: Heck, no. We can go back to being ego-based and uptight and defended anytime we like, because that's actually what we're programmed to be like both causally and primally. So we can go back any time. But the thing about practice is if we practise something for long enough, it becomes a default pattern. So by default, I've been open for about 25 to 30 years because I've practised it so intensely for some time before that, until it became my default pattern. Before that, I was closed by default pattern and had been for about 30 years.
S: Where do you think love comes from?
V: If I shut my eyes and go in, there's just vast nothingness, just vast nothingness. Now, if I open my eyes and come out, there's love. It's related to being out here, I guess, more than anything else. It's not just humans. When love's present, you love the flowers, the floor, the ceiling, the air, you love the air-conditioning. It's the funniest thing because I'm using English to describe this and it's very difficult because love is not personal. It just is, and it just loves.

When we use the "I" and say, "I love the..." the "I" in fact is not capable of love because the "I" is a dream. It's not real. It's a thought. Love is real, but the "I" is not. It's made up from imagination, but the "I" claims love when it experiences love. Love is actually impersonal and it just loves.

S: When you were talking about how you gave up everything, I wondered, how were you okay with that?

V: Yeah, I got to see that things don't make you happy. You know, I retired when I was 28 years old. Didn't have to work anymore, drove a Rolls Royce, had a penthouse in Peppermint Grove, and it does not make you happy. I got everything that everybody wanted. Does not make you happy. It's actually hollow. It's a con, because if you've desired your whole life to be successful, it doesn't stop. That's your default pattern. So even though you get everything, you're still desiring, which means you're still discontent. The only thing that I found that had contentment in it was love, and then ultimately Beingness. When the mind rests in Beingness, it's profoundly content for no reason: my ultimate definition of happiness.

S: When you were talking about the game of zero, I remembered that I always have a base level of resistance all of the time, not zero. So I wanted to ask you how to see the resistance more clearly so I can find zero.

V: I found the baseline of zero through the practice of meditation, sitting for long periods of time, until my mind stopped, and then I found zero, still conscious, still aware, but nothing happening. Zero. Meditation made zero obvious. But it also made everything else obvious as well. Meditation is how we get to see through the mind. We slow down and we watch. Become the witness. Okay?

~

V: Hello.

S: I was worried about making your tea because I didn't know if I'd stirred it enough. Then I didn't know if there was enough sugar.

V: I'd give that a 10 out of 10.

S: So then I just let go and surrendered. That's all I have.

V: Thank you for the tea. Is it time? It is time. Wow! Up on the back wall we've got the word "love" with a little heart on the end. That's so cool. But it's definitely not a word. It actually can't be described, but it can be perceived, and if you're willing to be open, you can start perceiving it. Unfortunately for most of us, including myself for so many years, I supported closure because it made me feel safe. There is no safety in the Way of the Heart because there is no safety in openness, and so in fact, we're going against the survival mechanism in serving Heart, but it's the Beauty Way.

Thank you for satsang. Good to see you bravehearts here today.

CHAPTER TWO

Finding Truth in the Era of New Age Spirituality

V: Welcome to satsang.
S: Hello, Vishrant. Can you please speak about the topic finding truth in the era of New Age spirituality?
V: New Age spirituality is in itself a kind of a religion and it is very mind-based, survival-orientated. Most of it's just smells and bells without any substance whatsoever, built on superstition and the gullibility of people. From Tarot readers through to channellers, people selling the idea of manifesting, people with the idea that there's some quickening happening. These are all just New Age ideas that have no basis in any form of reality.

People like to make money. There lies the problem with New Age spirituality because most of it has no substance whatsoever and it's easy for the charlatans to take advantage of the gullible. I don't have a great deal of time at all for New Age spirituality because people get lost in it. It's just another mind trip. Thinking somehow that they're going to get somewhere, probably being sold something. Truth, or what we truly are, has nothing to do with the mind, has nothing to do with manifesting, has nothing to do with channelling, has nothing to do with Tarot reading, has nothing to do with any of the smells and bells that wrap themselves around New Age spirituality.

Truth is pristine. Everything appears in it, and everything disappears in it. There is no separation in it. The true magic is just being – not anything else, just being. But most humans can't be. They live in their heads thinking, existing in a dream of projections to later and remembrance of the past and analysing what they think is problem solving. This is all rubbish because it's all just thought-based and thoughts aren't real. The same as the New Age religion is not real. It's thought-based. Truth is real. Beingness is real. Heart is real. What you think about it is not real.

There is some degree of reality in the ability to manifest, the ability to draw things in with the mind using energy, the manipulation and control of energy. That's more occultism though than New Age. It's been around forever and a day. Trying to take New Age ideas off people can be quite difficult, because they think they're real, but this whole game of higher consciousness is about stripping away the false, not about adding more false. You strip away everything that's in the way of higher consciousness. All belief systems, all ideologies, everything. All superstitions. All smells and bells. And you're left with what's real. You come to the present moment, and none of that stuff is real.

Switch on. Come to the present moment. Leave the mind behind. Be here now. This works.

Any questions? Any statements? Any challenges to this teaching today?

S: The first question. New Age spirituality tends to promote polyamory. Do you think people who do this are spiritual?
V: Promote what?
S: Polyamory?
V: Heck, what's polyamory?
S: I think it's like polygamy?
V: I have no idea. I don't understand the word. I'd need a definition of the word before I can answer that question. What's the question again?
S: So New Age spirituality tends to promote polygamy. Do you think people who do this –
V: Hang on a second. Does it? Do people in the New Age promote polygamy? I think that's a follow up fallacy in itself. The next part of the question?
S: The next part was "do you think people who do this are spiritual"?
V: Spiritual? I don't even like the word. You either go for Truth or you go for rubbish. If you're going for Truth, come to the present moment. Be present to what is real. Who we are, what we are, has nothing to do with the mind, has nothing to do with the body. Before the body was born, we were, and we are now. Find that that is aware. Find that that is eternal, that's always here, and then you've found your own true self. Polygamy, the idea, it's just sexuality, wanting to have sex with more than one partner. There's nothing particularly wrong with it, but it's not going to raise your consciousness levels. It's all lower chakra stuff.

~

S: Can crystals help with higher consciousness?
V: Crystals can be used as amplifiers for amplifying energy. They're used in radio sets. I remember when I was a kid, I made a crystal radio set. So they're good amplifiers. But most people are so scattered in the way they think, with their emotionality. They probably wouldn't be able to use crystals properly anyway. To use a crystal to focus anything, you'd need to have a very, very focused mind first.

~

S: The next question. What is the most common misconception about Enlightenment?
V: The most common misconception is that you become enlightened. That's the most common. That's not a possibility, because you as an "I" are basically a figment of your own imagination. Without imagination, you as an "I" cannot exist. What we are is real. Pure awareness. Pure consciousness. Real. The "I" can never ever wake up. It's not real. Awareness becomes aware of itself inside of a human being and stays aware of itself. That's Enlightenment. It has nothing to do with ego. As a matter of fact, when that occurs, the ego gets out of the way. It drops. It's seen clearly for what it is: a fake, a fraud.

~

S: Do you think that there are angels or entities that are here to guide us towards Enlightenment?
V: I have to put that in the I-don't-know column. I just don't know. I think it's quite possible that there are entities here, noncorporeal, but I don't know. It seems like there might be.

S: And is it helpful to try to connect to them?
V: No. People assume that because they come in contact with an entity that the entity is wise or has their best interests at heart. How would they know that? They assume that there's enlightened masters out there who are coming through as channels. I doubt that very much. If entities do exist, they're an energy form, and like all energy forms, including human beings, they need food, they need energy to survive. Humans eat food and turn it into energy to survive. Entities need energy as well to survive. If anything, the entities that are around live off the suffering of human beings because it's a high energy form.

S: The next question: what do you think of Sadhguru?
V: Well, I don't. I haven't met him. I haven't sat with him. I've listened to a very, very brief talk that he gave once years and years ago. He could very well be awake. I don't know. I have no attraction whatsoever to other awake teachers. He seems very intelligent. He seems to say the right things, but I don't know. Until you actually sit with someone and feel the energy field they're putting out, you don't know. He could very well be awake. He could very well be a great teacher. I just don't know. If you haven't sat with someone, if you haven't been in their presence, you don't know. Because anyone can pretend to be awake. Anyone can have the right mannerisms, say the right things, but that doesn't make them awake. It just means they're good at saying the right things, having the right mannerisms. Someone who's awake has a Buddha field around them 24 hours a day, seven

days a week. That's how you can tell if someone's awake. And with Sadhguru, he may very well be, I don't know. I haven't sat in his presence.

~

S: Vishrant, how are you? I had a question, but it's just totally gone away. Whenever I'm listening to you, it just completely blows me away. Such an honour to talk to you? Oh, yes. I'm in. . . .

V: When I was the seeker, I just wanted to talk to my teachers because I was aware of the energy field they were carrying and I was in love with that energy field. And so I understand wanting to talk to someone who's awake. I really do. I was the guy who always had my hand up. Always.

S: I know, I've actually been working on myself quite a lot. I mean, swimming in cold water in the sea to help the trauma like in Vancouver, and five, six-degree water every day. You suggested cold showers and instead I've just been snorkelling in the sea without a wetsuit for two months. And yeah, it just seems to be helping with releasing all of the trauma and everything. But my question is this, this connection that I'm feeling right now with you, is just blowing my whole body away. How would I be able to connect to you, to this, when I'm away working or something like that, so that I don't have to just be on this call asking you questions?

V: Okay. So when I was with Bhagwan Shree Rajneesh, as a sannyasin, I had a mala with his picture on it. Anytime I wanted to feel him, I would look at the picture on the mala and it would tune me in

because I was already in love with him. I was already connected with him. I was one of his sannyasins. And to tune into him, to connect with him, I'd just hold my mala and go quiet and look at it and it connected me in. Because we think of distance as reality, but Beingness is everywhere, and we are that. So there's no such thing as distance. Like, you're in Vancouver and I'm in Perth, Western Australia, and we're connected. That's at least 10,000 kilometres. There's no distance in Beingness. All you've got to do is tune in.
S: Okay, thank you. Thank you so much. I'll do that.
V: With your story about the water, the ocean, that was my thing as well. I loved being in the ocean. And I snorkelled. I got my C-class licence as a diver using tanks when I was 10 years old. I was absolutely fascinated by the ocean. I considered it the healing mother. Because it does. It takes all of the energy off you. It takes all of the darkness out of you, I agree.
S: Oh, oh, it's been amazing. I mean, I can't even tell you. I've been going down every day. It's like something … something's been calling me to go into the water. And sometimes I've been going as long as 30 minutes, which is too long. I almost got hypothermia the other day. So I've been averaging around about 10 minutes in five-to-six degree water. And I've been putting my head under as well. And it seems to just be sucking all of the trauma out of my system. It's unbelievable.
V: I'm very happy for you Peter. The thing about trauma is: don't repeat it. One of the things with trauma is usually it has belief systems around it and those belief systems actually protect it and keep it

going. And the main belief system that keeps it going is victim-oriented thinking, thinking you're ever a victim of anything. And so those things need to be undone as well.

S: Thank you. Thank you. I can feel your energy so strongly today. So, something's working. Thank you very much for your time.

V: Nice to talk to you, Peter. Enjoy your filming.

S: Thank you, sir. Thanks Vishrant.

~

S: Hello, Vishrant.

V: Hello Neil.

S: Yeah, so my question is like, when you were under the presence of your spiritual teachers, like, did you completely agree with everything that was shared by your teachers, or were there certain things that you disagreed with?

V: I didn't have a problem at all with Bhagwan Shree Rajneesh. I never, ever found a disagreement in what he was saying or what he was doing. I understood that he would contradict himself from time to time, but that was because he was talking to someone different in a different moment. And so it was appropriate what he was doing in that moment. With some of my Advaita Vedanta teachers, I wasn't completely impressed with some of their behaviours, but because they had the energy field, the Buddha field, I knew that in that field of energy I could dissolve and I could find myself as Truth. And so, with those particular teachers who weren't always walking their talk, so to speak, I would just sit in their presence and allow myself to expand and find myself as the everythingness, the nothingness, because they had the energy field.

When I examined how they were living their lives, I noticed that sometimes they were suffering. Someone who's fully enlightened doesn't suffer because they're surrendered. So, they hadn't really come completely home yet. They're on the way, but somewhere they were caught, possibly in money, possibly in sexuality, possibly in power. There was a little bit of work that they still needed to do to let go of things, but it didn't worry me even though I could see that. It didn't worry me because I could feel the Buddha field around them when I was with them in satsang and I knew how precious that was, how valuable that was for me as a seeker. It dissolved my coping mechanisms, it allowed my mind to expand, it opened my crown chakra, my third eye, my Heart. It was brilliant.

S: And there are certain things even when I listen to Osho that I find hard to grasp – like the concept of karma, reincarnation, chakras – because I've never experienced these things, so how should I approach these things?

V: Anything that is not your own direct experience, approach with doubt, and put it in the maybe column. So don't discount it completely. Put it in the maybe column. This is the approach I had to everything regarding spirituality because there's so much absolute bulldust in spirituality. You've got to approach it with doubt. If something's not your own direct experience, your own direct knowing, put it in the doubt

column. And this is the way of the seeker to find out for themselves, to not believe anything. The moment we start believing things. We are lost. We're imprisoned by beliefs. Doubt. Doubt everything. Doubt me. Correct. Doubt me. Find out for yourself. Look where I'm pointing. Find out for yourself.
S: Alright, yep, that was it. Thank you, Vishrant.

~

S: Hi Bhagwan. Somebody just asked you about using crystals and you said you would have to learn to focus your energies. What does that mean "focus your energies"? Is that the same as focusing your mind?
V: Yeah, in a way. So a person wants something. Say they want a new car and they decide that they want to draw that in through manifestation. So they put up a thing inside their mind, "I want that new car," and they focus on "they want the new car" and they focus on the colour of the car, the type of car, the year of the car, the condition of the car. So, they're getting quite a strong focus happening on what they want. At the same time, they may be running a fear, like, "Oh, I might not be able to get that, I might not have enough money, I might not have this, I might not have that." So, fear comes into play. Now they're so scattered. Any form of manifesting they're doing is not going to work. If you want something and you want to use the mind to get it in the form of manifesting, you have to just want that. You can't have any other side thoughts, taking it apart, dismissing it, diminishing it. You can't be scattered. You have to be focused.

S: Would that work for wanting Beingness?

V: Wanting Beingness won't bring you Beingness, but what it will do is it'll put you in a position where you're willing to do what it takes to find it. So without that want of Beingness or without that thirst for Beingness, it's probably not going to happen because the price is pretty high. You have to sacrifice you.

S: Yes. So merely manifesting for things is . . . that's not what seekers are about. Are we?

V: No, that's right. I'll answer just about any question that people ask me.

S: I'll ask you a question just to talk to you. Thank you so much Bhagwan.

V: Nice to talk to you, Susha.

S: Likewise, always. Thank you.

~

S: Hello Bhagwan. Bhagwan, is chanting, singing bajans, any kind of help? Are they helpful?

V: They can be in that they can bring your mind to a single point, particularly if it's a repetitive bajan. On the other hand, most bajans are also devotional, they're usually singing the praises of God or something like that. That can ignite the Heart and can open the mind and open the Heart. And so they do work.

S: There are some songs which are not exactly spiritual songs, they are movie songs, but they do make me feel good and feel open.

V: Well, anything that opens you up and allows you to perceive love is worthy, basically. Love is the true jewel of consciousness. It's beautiful.

S: Thank you.

~

S: Hello Vishrant, I wanted to share an experience that I had. And I just wanted to get your take on it, if you could? So the other night, I had laid down, was getting ready for bed, trying to fall asleep, and I started focusing on my breathing. And then I don't know, maybe five or 10 minutes into it I was completely relaxed. And all of a sudden, my awareness, it's like the power to my mind, it's like somebody had unplugged my mind. It was just, poof! Gone. And I was aware that it was gone. And I don't think it lasted more than a few minutes because I panicked and like I thought, "Oh my god, am I having a stroke? Like, where'd my mind go?" I lost my mind. It was so profound. It was completely just off. And so I was just curious, you know, what would you make of it? Of something like that?

V: Okay, so I started meditating formally when I was 28 years old and it didn't take me that long to start finding no-mind, where I was there, but the mind wasn't there. And that's when the quest for Enlightenment began because I realised I was there, but the mind wasn't there. So therefore, I couldn't be the mind. And if I'm not the mind, what am I? What am I really? And eventually the understanding was that that was aware of the mind was my own true nature, and that's what needed to find itself. And so, you got a taste of no-mind and the beauty of that and it sounded like it was a pretty profound event for you. That's great. Now the question is:

what's aware? What's aware of the no-mind? What's aware of the mind? What's aware of the thoughts? What's aware of the space between the thoughts? "What's aware?" is the question because what's aware is who we are.

S: Yeah, yeah, it was. Yeah, definitely. I mean, when in the sitting, in meditation, and sometimes you have those little brief gaps, you know? And so that had been as far as my experience with little, little tiny little milliseconds of no-mind, I guess. But this was certainly more, and yeah ... so, next time, yeah. Let's see if there is a next time hopefully. There will be, as we practise to just not panic.

V: It's also possible you're experiencing a small satori where awareness was aware of itself to some degree. Just keep looking. Just keep looking at the same space. Witness the mind. Self-inquire. Relax. It always happens in a relaxed mind. It never happens in an uptight mind. Relaxed mind is the way to go. See if you can't find that rising in love.

S: That's my mission.

V: As a Sikh, you're a disciple. And the aim of the disciple is to know themselves as Truth.

S: And love it. Thank you so much Vishrant, I'll just go with, with yep, we're gonna keep going.

V: Bye bye, Aaliyah.

~

S: Hello, Vishrant. I can't quite understand why me as awareness cannot perceive what others do. Is consciousness somewhat localised in the body?

V: Ask the question again.

S: I can't quite understand why me as awareness cannot perceive what others do. Is consciousness somewhat localised in the body?

V: Ask the first part of the question again.

S: I can't quite understand why me as awareness cannot perceive what others do.

V: I think you're projecting onto awareness. Awareness is our nature. I think you're talking about the awareness of the mind, not awareness as in Beingness. I think there's a misunderstanding here. Ask the whole question again.

S: I can't quite understand why me as awareness cannot perceive what others do. Is consciousness somewhat localised in the body?

V: Pure awareness is everywhere. It is the mind that does the interpreting. It is the mind that does the analysing. It's the mind that witnesses and records it. But pure awareness doesn't do anything. It just is. And we are that. I think there's some confusion here.

~

S: There's another question by Mona. Does age or ageing have an impact on Enlightenment?

V: Not on Enlightenment. On the mind and the body, it does. Not on Enlightenment. Pure awareness is not touched by anything because it's never born and it cannot die. And so there is no detriment to Enlightenment with age. The mind itself finds it harder to change default patterns as it gets older because its default patterns are hardwired for longer. And some of those default patterns may be in the way of Enlightenment, in the way of Heart, and so they're harder to change. They say that it's hard to teach old dogs new tricks. While there's a certain truth in that, it's absolutely possible if you persevere.

As far as what happens in Enlightenment, as you get older, the mind tends to disappear more and more and more. You'll find that it's not there very often, because we're not the mind, we're pure Beingness. We're always here. Everyone's at their final destination. They just don't know it, because they're not aware of it. What they're aware of is the mind, and then the mind suffers, projects, remembers, analyses – and people think they're that, but that's not who we are. It's not what we are. We're that that's aware of the mind. We're that that is simply aware. And we are always here.

S: You mentioned that the price for Enlightenment is sacrificing yourself. Did you ever regret in any shape or form making that sacrifice or do you even now see it as a sacrifice after Enlightenment?

V: I don't see it as a sacrifice now, not at all, and I have never ever for a moment had a regret at the decision my mind made to basically give itself in unconditional surrender to Truth or God. And it died. It was 22 years ago, coming at the end of this May. I died. And there hasn't been anybody here since. There's a sense of nothing here, nobody here, whereas before awakening there was always a sense of somebody doing something. Now, there's no sense of somebody being here or doing anything and there's no regret because that thing that died, the Vishrant that died, wasn't who I was, and it was basically like everybody else, a suffering machine, constantly desiring things to be different than how they are or were, and being attached to the things that it thought it had and being fearful of losing them. Well, that all went. That was really good. But as long as you think that you're an "I", you're caught in that. You're caught in desires and attachments. You're caught in suffering. The only freedom from that is to know self as Truth – for awareness to turn on itself and stay aware of itself. That is freedom from knowing yourself as a mind, knowing yourself as a body, which is a prison, actually, the bars of which are made of fear. So definitely no regrets. But that's from the mind's perspective. From Beingness's perspective, nothing matters. Never does because it doesn't judge.

S: Okay, good to hear. I mean, from the mind's perspective, I'm still way too identified with the mind. It really feels like dying.

V: It is. That's what happens. You go towards Enlightenment, and you as an "I" die. That's actually what happens. And that's why terror can arise because terror is just a defensive act on the mind's behalf to protect it.

S: So is meditation like, you just gradually ease into it so that it's not like a shock to the system, or ... ?

V: I'd say that's true. I started meditating when I was 28 and started finding no-mind and realising that, well, I wasn't mind, I couldn't be. I was just here and there was no-mind here. There was no thinking. And so yeah, that definitely helped when it came to the ultimate surrender, knowing full well that what was surrendering, what was dying, had nothing to do with who I was, not really . . . or "what I was" is a better way of putting it.

S: Okay, thank you for clarifying this.

V: Yeah, you're very welcome. Good question. Thank you.

~

S: The next question is from Peter.

V: Back again.

S: Sorry, Vishrant. I'm being greedy today. I'm just . . . I'm just wanting to ask, actually in continuation with what Rajesh was saying in the chat before, there seems to be a point where what we are meditating on starts meditating me. Like, this energy that I'm feeling in my body now when I'm talking to you, it comes over me sometimes, but to a lesser extent, while I'm working, whatever, and I'm aware that it's kind of pulling me into the present moment and my mind just stops. And how – maybe if I can formulate this into a question – how can I integrate that very powerful energy into everything I do so that it uses everything that I am to, to just flow in the present moment, if you know what I mean?

V: The funny thing is, Peter, it already does. That's the cosmic joke. We just think we have control. We just think that we can do things. Everything is God. Everything is being done by God. Everything.

S: Yeah, yes. And it seems to be like little tightening loops that come back again and again, and I'm finding that they sometimes are very, very painful because I think then, I don't know, they feel like they almost mixed up with it. Old trauma and old, old, whatever . . . I was saying the cold water seems to be helping my brain with it. But just to stay in that point is so hard. With you, it's unbelievably easy, like I'm here now and I'll be buzzing for hours and hours after I talk to you. But without that, whether, you know, it's like I'm plugged into a battery charger talking to you, but after this, Oh man, I'm on my own again. And then those demons come back, especially early in the morning to haunt me. And I have to just sit with them like, okay, and don't chase them away. Just sit with them. It's like an onion. There's layers and layers.

V: Okay, so I can tell you this. One of my teachers who I never met, but I studied Papaji, the Advaita Vedanta teacher, a disciple of Ramana Maharshi. Papaji, when he was younger, was in the military, and at night time, he used to dress up in women's clothes and dance for Krishna because he was so devoted to Krishna. And I always found that quite funny until I actually had a look at my own life and recognised what facilitated Enlightenment. And it was really quite simple. I gave God my suffering. I gave God my pleasures. I gave God absolutely everything and left nothing in my hands.

S: Thank you so much. Thank you. That's what I'm going to do is when that comes, I'm just going to give it back, just . . . just give it, give it back. Thank you. Thank you, I really appreciate that.

V: Thank you, Peter.

~

S: The next question is from Deepesh.

V: Hello Deepesh.

S: Hello. Namaste. My question is that I try to be aware more and more. Last year I talked to you, and it is more and more threatening because I'm applying the things, but one thing is keeping me confused, which is that when I practise sometimes, when I am not aware, it is my mind completely overtakes me. But I realised later, after 15 minutes or 20 minutes, that it has completely overtaken me. And sometimes some fear comes, and again, I tried to be conscious. So, what should I do in this condition? I should just, it is okay, that I am driven by the mind because sometimes it goes for hours?

V: Yeah. It doesn't matter how many times you fail. What matters is how many times you try again. Because it's in failing that we learn. We learned how to walk by failing. We didn't learn by successes, but by failing. And when it comes to higher consciousness and turning awareness onto itself or even being present to what is real, we learn by practice and we learn by failures. Never give yourself a hard time for failing. It is okay. Accept the failure and try again. Be kind to yourself.

S: Okay, okay. And I have another question that is just a curiosity, which is that whenever I am practising, I find "me" as a part of the story, and everything is turning around. So, is it normal that that is turning around, it is taking every time, me, as a part of the story, and it is going revolving, revolving and I am dreaming. Suddenly, I think, "Oh, it is not so, it is the problem".

V: That is the mind.

What is aware of that is of relevance. What is aware of that occurring? That is relevant. What the mind does is irrelevant. What's aware of that happening? Follow, follow the "I" thought back to the source. What is aware of the mind doing what it's doing? Whatever the mind does is irrelevant. But what's aware of that, that's important. What's this that is always aware, that is always here? What's this?

S: Okay, thank you. Thank you so much.

V: Thank you.

~

S: The next question is from Tyagna.

V: Hi, Tyagna.

S: Hello. Hi, Vishrant.

V: Have you been causing trouble for your mother-in-law again?

S: I don't even know when I've caused trouble. So, I just had a question like, I've watched my cat every day. And I see that he's very, like, present in the moment, and I think that's the case with all animals. So is it that they're, like part of Beingness or something like, like you say that consciousness is everywhere? So, are they connected to that?

V: Well, animals don't tend to dream like humans, they tend to be more present. Wild animals in particular, like foxes or wolves, are very, very present animals. You find that animals like cows and sheep aren't so present.

But if we really want to live this life totally and fully, we need to become like a wolf or a fox: very present, present to what is real, and then we're living in reality instead of living in a dream in our minds.

S: Yeah, so the problem, I guess the problem with humans is obviously the brain, the mind, that makes us dream. And animals don't have that because they don't have the capacity to think like us.

V: No. But as humans, we can become very present to reality as well. Because our lives are so safe and so comfortable, we tend to live in our thoughts, in dream. But if we're going to raise our consciousness levels, we need to get back to being more present to what is real rather than present to dream.

S: Yeah, I feel that when I ... when I'm in your presence, but then it goes away.

V: Ah.

S: It goes away. And sometimes ... sometimes I do feel it on my own. If I'm, like, I've noticed sometimes if I'm walking by myself, just in nature, it sometimes happens that I have experienced no-mind.

V: It's not necessarily experiencing no-mind. I'm talking about being present to what is real. I don't know what's around you at the moment, but whatever is in front of you is real. What you think about it is not. So, when we put all of our awareness on what is in front of us and what we hear, we're putting our awareness on what is real. If we're thinking about it, we're lost in dream.

S: Yeah, but that's the issue. Like, if I'm looking around, like, let's say, I'm looking at a tree, I will have some thought about it, like, "Oh, it's such a beautiful tree". And then that's when I'm not in reality anymore.

V: That's right, you've left reality. It's like watching a sunset and then commenting on it. The moment you comment on it, you've left reality to some degree because you've started dreaming about the sun.
S: Yeah, exactly that. It's also just the chattering of the mind because I have a lot of energy and I'm very talkative. And that sort of, I guess it's just, I don't know if it makes me think too much.
V: No. If you practise being present to reality, you can still be very talkative. Just you'll be more present to reality like a wolf rather than a sheep.
S: Yeah, like me like redirecting my energy, I think.
V: Well, direct your energy towards what is real rather than towards what is not.
S: Yeah, thank you Vishrant. I had another question too. So, you see that everything is karmic.
V: Okay.
S: And I always wonder like, what is karmic? Like, is it our actions? Is it our words? Is it our thoughts?
V: All of those things, all of them, everything. Our thoughts, our words or actions, there's always karma involved in them. Whatever we put into life we get back, and so when you're around your mother-in-law, you should be a little bit quieter because your loudness disturbs her. She came on the other day and had a bit of a complaint about you. I hear you're moving out soon.
S: Yes, I am. I think that's best for all of us.
~
S: The next question is from Shyena.
V: Hi, Shyena.

S: Hi Vish. If I'm being completely honest with myself –

V: Oh my god, you mean sometimes you're not?

S: Sometimes I'm in denial.

V: I love it when people say things like that "if I'm being completely honest". Well, does that indicate that a lot of the time you're not being honest?

S: Possibly, that my beloved is, is within me, and I am the love that I seek.

V: But they're ideas. Ideas aren't real. They're not reality.

S: The love that I feel when I'm in deep presence, that love is real.

V: That's real, yes. But what you think about it's not. There's the problem, because we have trouble discerning the difference between what is real and what is not. And nothing you think is real. Love is real.

S: Is it, is it a default pattern or belief system or both?

V: You've practised living in your head like the rest of us who went to school. You've practised living in your head, so you live in your head. You live in thoughts rather than reality because that's what you've practised.

S: That sometimes has the power to bring the thought that love is outside of us?

V: Say that again, that last bit?

S: That love is outside of us, is it?

V: Well in fact, you know, in a way, from the mind's perspective, from the I's perspective, it is outside because the "I" sees everything as outside. That's duality. The mind sees itself as separate from everything. But that's not the Truth. The Truth is we are everything. We're not separate at all. But the mind sets itself up as something that is separate even though it's not.

S: Okay. Would you say that love is the highest vibration?

V: Vibrations appear in Beingness. And so when we're talking about high and low, you can't talk about them in Beingness because Beingness is everything. You can't have polarities in Beingness. You can't have any form of duality in Beingness, not really, because it's everything. So when you talk about a higher or lower vibration in Beingness? Everything is Beingness. Everything is Beingness, and so you're still thinking in forms of duality when you're talking about high and low. You're still looking at things from the perspective of duality. We are non-dual. We are everything.

S: I had an experience quite a while back now, but it was after meditation where just this overwhelming sensation of love that I don't think it'd be possible to function, it was that intense, and I haven't experienced it like that since, but –

V: That's because you're not used to it. I'm sure you could get used to it.

S: Absolutely.

V: Love is beautiful and it's actually always here. It's just that we cut ourselves off from the perception of it through our defendedness, through our closures, our resistance to life. It's always here. It's always beautiful. Depends what your mind was being affected by as well as love at the time.

S: Nothing. No external substance. Thank you, Vishrant.
V: Nice talking to you, Shyena.

~

S: The following question is from a viewer: Is it okay to lie sometimes?
V: Okay to lie sometimes? Now we're working into right, wrong, good and bad. It's not a world I live in. I live in "whatever is" is – whatever it is, is meant to be, otherwise it wouldn't be so. I don't live in this world of right, wrong, good and bad. That's the world of "let's suffer". I live in a world where everything is happening as it's meant to be happening, otherwise it wouldn't be happening. In that world, my mind rests. There's no tension, there's no uptightness when things perceivably go wrong because it's meant to be so, otherwise it wouldn't be happening.

Everything's cool. You're cool. Once the mind masters the idea of acceptance, it can truly relax. Acceptance is the way we learn unconditional surrender. But it's not that practised, but it should be, because it's a cure-all of everything. Once you accept life as it is, life is beautiful.

Thank you for satsang. Good to see you bravehearts here today.

CHAPTER THREE

How to Deal with Uncertainty

S: Hello Vishrant, can you please speak about today's topic, how to deal with uncertainty?
V: You know, everyone wants everything to be certain, but that's just not the reality of the world we live in. Nothing is really certain except that we're going to die. Everything else is up for grabs. And so the truth is, life is uncertain, and as a result, unsafe in a lot of ways. And we scramble for safety, we scramble to make sure that everything's okay, and in doing so, create stress for ourselves, or we hermit ourselves away from life, not being in life because there's too much danger, too much uncertainty. But really, if we want to live totally, we need to be able to be okay with the unknown. We need to be okay with uncertainty. We need to step through our fears rather than serve them.

So sure, life's uncertain. You don't know what's going to happen when you get into a car with someone. You're driving, someone could hit you, there could be a drunk driver or someone who's stoned out there or someone who's just dangerous. We really don't know what's going to happen next. We project that everything's going to be somehow okay. But we don't know. And we don't know if our family is really going to be safe. We do our best to make them safe, but are they really going to be safe? We don't know. There is so much uncertainty, and if we can be okay with that uncertainty then we can relax. But if we can't be okay with that uncertainty, we cannot relax. We stay in a state of tension. But we're doing it to ourselves because the world is the way the world is. It's not going to change because we worry or get disturbed. Nothing changes. And so all of that effort into worrying is a waste of time.

In a lot of ways, we create our reality by how we think. And if we're serving fear, well, we're not creating a very nice life for ourselves. If we can be okay with life as it is, if we can be more fatalistic – what happens is meant to happen – we can have quite a nice life, a relaxed life, a life that is more in line with higher consciousness rather than suffering. But that's up to you because you create your reality by the way you think. Uncertainty is just a part of reality. It's just how it is. We don't know, and can you be okay with not knowing? Or are you going to try to make everything so safe that you're dead before the body even dies? Up to you. If you really want to have a lot of fun in this life, step through your fears, don't serve them. Don't serve them at all, okay?

Are there any questions, any statements, any challenges to anything that's been said today?
S: The first question is: I'm looking for work at the moment and I noticed that I run a low level of anxiety. My practice is to discount the negative thoughts and the worry. Is that enough to go back to zero permanently?

V: Okay, so the negative thoughts are probably frightened of losing something. There's probably some loss involved: not getting the job, maybe not being able to meet commitments. And so you'll need to have a look at that. What is it that you don't want to lose? The moment you become willing to accept the loss, you have a certain level of freedom. But as long as you're holding against that loss, you've got stress, you've got turmoil, you've got a problem. You're creating the problem. Life is just the way it is. You don't know if you're going to get a job or you're not going to get a job. You do your best. Be okay with loss and you can relax. Be okay with letting go and you can relax. You can't relax while you're holding on. Not possible. There's a tension in it.

S: Is being okay with loss the same as practising imagining losing what you don't want to lose?

V: Could be. It could be. An extreme example of that is: I've been a diver, underwater diver most of my adult life. As a matter of fact, I got my C-class licence for diving with tanks when I was 10 years old. And I've always been – in the past before awakening – I was always frightened of sharks because I had a certain level of trauma around sharks that had been created by direct experience of having a relative mauled to death by a shark. So every time I went in the water, there was always this fear of sharks, particularly because I dived in waters where there were lots of sharks. The western end of Rottnest Island off Western Australia, there's lots of sharks. The Abrolhos Islands, there's lots of sharks. And so what

I would allow myself to do before I'd actually get in the water, is I'd make it okay for the sharks to maul me in my own mind. I'd just make it okay. I'd make it okay to die, and in practising that, in allowing the fear to come about rather than resisting it, fear lost its power because I wasn't feeding it anymore with resistance. I'd moved to acceptance. I'd moved to okayness. Now that's a pretty extreme example of dealing with fear, but we can deal with fear the same way. All fears. We just allow the worst to happen in our minds and fear then loses its power because it's not being resisted. But that's up to you. You try it and see. For me, it worked well as a diver because the fear of dying, of being eaten by sharks or being mauled by sharks, could have put me off diving altogether, but it didn't because I made it okay. I made it okay. What do you make okay?

S: It sounds like you turned this hobby of diving into a spiritual practice.

V: Not deliberately, but it turns out that way, yes.

When we practise dying or when we practise that level of let-go, we are preparing the mind for higher consciousness. We are preparing the mind to overcome the survival mechanism that's in the way of Enlightenment. So even though I didn't know what I was doing, as far as the spiritual practice was concerned, when I look back on it, in hindsight, I can clearly see that because I was diving every weekend for years and years and years and years, and that was a practice, at some point it became very easy for me to just let go because I'd practised a lot. People can get the idea of let-go intellectually, but that doesn't change much in the psyche. You have to practise it. And if you practise, whatever you practise, you will get good at it. So I got good at letting go of my life and that allowed me to have such an adventurous life. I didn't let fear get in my way. I went for it, and lived totally, squeezed the juice out of life as a result, rather than played it safe. I never really expected to live past the age of 20 because I lived such an exciting life. I was into extreme sports, motorbike racing, car rallying, rugby, martial arts, deep sea diving, hunting – all sports that involved a risk. I wasn't about to let fear rule my life. I could see clearly that when you let fear rule your life, you don't have much fun. You move out of flow and into stuck.

~

S: Hey, Bhagwan. So, you were diving into the ocean with sharks, you made it okay. I have a fear of snakes. I'm going nowhere near snakes, nothing is happening. Should I still use this technique of imagining being attacked by snakes or something like that and be okay with it?

V: If you wish to, it just reminded me of a story that happened to me once. I also had a fear of snakes because snakes in Australia are quite deadly, most of them. We've got lots of poisonous snakes here that have the ability to kill you reasonably quickly. And I was going through a stage of my life where I was studying shamanism with a shaman, and he discovered that I had this fear of snakes. And we came across a big Brown snake in the orchard that had been living in a rock grove with reeds and things around it, and it was a big Brown snake, very deadly. And he said, "I'd like you to go down and sleep with that snake tonight. I'd like you to go down and lay in that area and just sleep there". And being as crazy as I have been in this life, I went down and I slept with a snake that night. When I say slept, I didn't sleep a wink. I was awake all night, listening to see if there was any movement or anything that touched me. But it was incredible because as the night went on, and I got tireder and tireder and tireder, the surrender in me got deeper and deeper and deeper. And really, the only thing that we need to get enlightened is unconditional surrender. Anything you can do that allows you to learn acceptance, allows you to learn surrender, is worthy.

So whatever you do, even if it's in your dreams, practise let-go, practise acceptance, practise surrender because this is the key to higher consciousness. This is the key to the awakening of the Heart. This is the key to awakening to Beingness, unconditional surrender.
S: Thank you.
V: Oh by the way, I don't recommend anyone ever sleep with a snake. That was just me being really, really silly.
S: Thank you for clarifying that. I thought I was going to go sit in the park next to the snakes.
V: No, there are some things I did that I look back on and I go, "Geez!"
S: Would you say that this is the same, this technique of imagining a loss, is also a way to deal with attachments?

V: Ah, you mean letting go of things that you're attached to?

S: Yeah, people, family members, children – is this the way to let go of the attachment, to imagine the worst?

V: With attachments, it's a little different. I found it's funny with attachments because I never really let go of anything except smoking cigarettes. Everything gave me up as my consciousness levels rose, so it wasn't that I let things go, I found that everything let me go. The only thing that I really had trouble giving up and did need to give up was smoking cigarettes, and I did that some 40 years ago. And it was ridiculous. The reason I gave them up was because I had trained as a naturopath and I thought to myself, you can't work as a naturopath giving people advice on health when you're smoking cigarettes. So I gave up smoking cigarettes.

S: What about people you were close to?

V: No, never really gave them up. They . . . things dropped away. As my consciousness levels rose, things just dropped away. Like up until nearly awakening, I used to like a glass of wine, a merlot or something like that. I grew up in a family where we all drank for meals and drank alcohol for meals. And I found that one day I just didn't feel like it anymore. I just didn't want anymore, just didn't want to have another drink. It gave me up. But consciousness levels were pretty high. This was just before Enlightenment.

S: When we use the technique like imagining, is there a fear of getting more into the dream?

V: There is, but imagining it can help us in lots of ways. We can heal some of our wounding by imagining. We can learn to be tenderly okay with ourselves by imagining, particularly if we get involved in doing the inner child work which is all imagination. It's quite a powerful tool for learning to love and accept parts of yourself that have been put aside, that have been neglected or been ignored. So imagination is definitely a powerful tool in healing. But it's also a powerful tool in stepping through fear, if we want to. If we want to. Imagining the worst to occur and making it okay, it gives us a lot of freedom.
S: Thank you.

~

S: Hi Vishrant. So I had a question about attachments and primal bonding. So when I strip everything away that I think I would absolutely be left with, if I were able to strip away all the rest, it would be my children and mom.
V: Yeah.
S: And then with my mom ... it's quite complicated. How do we deal with this?
V: If you had a minute left to live, what would you hang on to?
S: My children and –
V: So imagine hanging on to your children in the last minute. How would that make you feel?
S: Desperate.
V: Yeah, really? Now do it again and imagine just loving them as you're dying. How does that feel?
S: Much better.

V: Yeah. You see, what we hang on to creates suffering. If we can just move from that to love, it changes completely. It actually changes into let-go because in true love, you'd hold on to nothing, because love just loves, it doesn't take prisoners, and love is way beyond primal bonding. You just love them.

S: Okay.

V: You try it and see. Practise. Just love them. If you only have that one minute left to live, what's the last gift you want to give them? Would it be your desperation or your love?

S: It's very clear.

V: Yeah. Yep.

S: Thank you.

~

S: Next, Marcus has written a question: Vishrant, sometimes I sense my true nature as Beingness, but at times, I think it's all in my imagination. How do I know if it's a true satori or just my imagination?

V: Okay, so the thing with imagination, the mind is capable of imagining all sorts of things. It can imagine love. It can imagine silence. It can imagine stillness. It can imagine emptiness. It can imagine nothingness. It even can imagine the infinite, Beingness, to some degree, but it gets stale. It can imagine the infinite, but it gets stale. The real deal is never stale, it's always fresh, and so the way to examine it and see if it's real or not is related to freshness. Is it fresh? Is it here now? Or is it something that's getting stale because it's a dream that you're having? A dream that's repetitive in some way. The mind is wonderful at imagining, and it can fool you, but just keep watching it. If it's the mind, it'll get stale. If it's the real deal, it will not. It's always fresh. Okay?

~

S: Hello, Vishrant. So my question is, everything that happens to us in life, is it already meant to happen or is it really uncertain events? Or is it leading us to somewhere?

V: I don't know. People love to know. They love to know the answer to things. But the truth is I don't know. I just don't know. I know that some people believe it is already written. I just don't know. I know that my mind runs true to the patterning that was put in it the same as yours does, the same as everyone else. And so I know it's going to do what it's programmed to do. But whether it's written or not, I just don't know. And the more you get to know, the more conscious you become, the more you realise you don't know. And the reason we want to know is because we want to somehow control things. But as your consciousness levels rise, that need to control things disappears. And so you become more honest. I don't know. I just don't know. Because you don't need to know anymore because you're not trying to control, you're not trying to survive anymore.

S: Right. And I remember in one of the previous satsangs, you mentioned that committing suicide is not karmically good. So why is it not karmically good?

V: Suicide is murder of an innocent body. Murder is not good, karmically.

S: Okay. Right, but yogis, sometimes they talk about leaving their bodies. Isn't that also just like ending life at their own will?

V: I understand what you're saying and I know that that's possible. Whether it's suicide or not, I don't know. You see, a yogi might know themselves as Truth, they might already be awake. And so it's not like they're really going anywhere. They're still there.

See, people think they are the mind and the body. We are not the mind and body. So once again it's a question where I don't know. I just don't know. People expect that people who are awake should know everything. Well, that's just rubbish. I don't know. There's so much I don't know.

S: Alright, thank you Vishrant.

~

S: Yeah, how are you? I'm from Dallas, Texas. Nice to be in satsang, really excited. So the question is, I intellectually understand, based on, you know, some of the spiritual practices I have undertaken so far. Like, I am not the person that I assumed to be, like a body or mind or anything like that, I'm something much beyond that. I'm pure consciousness, awareness, the Being, the living reality, unfiltered reality, and so on. However, it's said that if that sense of self doesn't drop or disappear, the illusion of the self is not seen through. You don't really feel or experience that moment to moment in our living reality, but intellectually understand it, but it is not happening for me, no matter what I do, it doesn't. The self is not dropping. It's almost like you had to do something else, like some intuition should arise, which is beyond the mind to see the self through, or should drop on its own, which is like kind of waiting for something to happen.

V: I do know the answer to what you're asking. Okay, so for me, I had a thousand satoris before awakening, and the "I" kept coming back. The self kept coming back. But after awakening, when awareness stayed aware of itself, the "I" dropped by itself. It just dropped. The mind could not in any way believe that it was real any longer because awareness was aware of itself. And so it dropped. It dropped as a result of Enlightenment or you could say satori that was continuing. But up until that point it kept coming back, it kept resurrecting itself.

S: Okay, so do the spiritual practices like meditation or self-inquiry, do they help? Some people say that they get in the way of dropping the self because they perpetuate the game of the self. It's just like, kind of boosting somebody's spiritual ego or something like that. They don't really help. Or some people say they do help.

I've seen evidence in both cases. I've seen some people wake up based on the things that they practised. Some people just got it spontaneously, they never did any spiritual practice at all or they never meditated for a single day. So I kind of wonder like, if there is some randomness to it, or is there a karmic effect, but there is nothing there?

V: The ego can use most spiritual practices to bolster itself because it starts thinking it's special, because it does meditation or does self-inquiry or does asanas. The only thing that I found, the only spiritual practice I found that the ego can't use to serve itself, or use to escape in, is the practice of openness.

S: Openness?

V: The practice of openness. Always being open. Anytime you close, you open up. The ego can't survive openness, because the ego itself is a contraction.

S: Ah, open meaning like open to experiences, open to whatever is happening in the present moment. Is that what it means?

V: No defences. No defence systems whatsoever. So no contractions, no resistance to anything.

S: Oh, okay. Okay. Got it. No resistance. Okay.

V: Yeah and that works. The ego cannot defeat openness. It cannot use openness to hide in. It cannot use openness in any way. Openness actually destroys the ego because the ego is a form of closure.

S: Right. It's a form of contracted energy, right?

V: That's correct. That's correct.

S: Okay, so okay, great. Thank you very much, sir.

~

S: Hi again Vishrant. Okay, question: I read a book called Many Lives, Many Masters by Dr Brian Weiss. Do you know that book?

V: No, I don't know it. I've heard of it, but I haven't read it.

S: Okay. Alright. So it just talks about past lives, and you know, just the concept, I think in the Western world, and I might be messing up sort of how I'm relaying this, but basically that, you know, we do have past lives. In the Western world, that's not such an accepted concept and relating to that, I was curious, do past lives set us up for this life as far as karma in our journey?

V: Okay, so what I know about past lives is I started remembering them when I was 12 years old. And I was in Catholic boarding school as a boarder. And I found myself basically as nothing. I was playing the part of a dragon's tail in a play on stage, and I just experienced self as an absolute nothing. I didn't know what had happened. They took me to the medical centre and they thought I'd hit my head, but I hadn't hit my head, I'd had a satori. And after that, I started remembering a previous life. I started remembering what I did. I started remembering my name. I started remembering the language that I used. I remembered how old I was. I remembered how I died. I was very young, and to me this was all rubbish because I was a Catholic and Catholics don't have past lives. But it persisted. It persisted into my 20s, and then into my 30s that particular memory kept resurrecting itself. And then in my 30s, about age 33, I started remembering all of the lives before that, and there were hundreds of them. People think, well, you remember your lives, and it's a good thing. Well no, you remember the highlights, and the highlights are usually the traumas. And so in most of my past lives I was either into spirituality as a monk or a priest, or I was a soldier, or I was both, and I remembered the battles, I remembered the bloodshed, I remembered the horrors. And what it gave me was: I don't want to do this again. I've been around the block too many times. It's time. It's time to stop this samsara, this cycle of birth, and what I would call suffering and death. Enlightenment is the ticket out of that because you die before the body does as an "I" and it doesn't come back again. So I'm talking to you, but there's no sense whatsoever of anyone here talking to you. The one who used to live here died 23 years ago. There's just talking now. Nobody talking.

S: Wow, okay. You've also spoken about the dark night of the soul. Can you elaborate on that a little bit?

V: It's a phrase used by Carl Jung, the very famous psychologist. It's about what happens when you finally allow yourself to feel what's underneath everything.

We develop a whole pile of defence systems to protect ourselves from feeling past wounding and past traumas and past damage, and we sit on this raft that we've created. We meet the world with it, which is part of our personality, but underneath this raft are all of the things we haven't dealt with. And as a person becomes willing to feel what's under there, what's under there comes out, or they may not be willing to feel what's under there and it comes out because of some kind of reaction to something. The dark night of the soul goes on until everything is emptied out, until all the wounds of the Heart have been healed.

I got in touch with that through the Rajneesh washing machine. The Mystery School that Osho Rajneesh was running, I was involved in that. I did, gosh, I did a lot of months, I think I did 15 or 16 months in Mystery School being undone and having everything emptied out. Then I went on and trained as a psychotherapist which was another "let's open you up and empty everything out" and everything got emptied out. But it's like an onion. You don't know how many layers there are. You get through one, you go "Whew, it's the end, thank God for that" and then there's another layer.

I had a quite traumatic childhood so there were quite a few layers of different repressed emotions, repressed traumas that needed to be released. So the dark night of the soul went on for a while, but I had a willingness to meet it. I had a willingness to be okay with it. That's what's required, a willingness. Unfortunately, you and I are programmed to avoid pain and chase pleasure or comfort, and that primal program goes against us healing the wounds of our Heart. But if you really want to heal the wounds, you just become willing to feel them. All that's required is your willingness to feel, rather than your willingness to avoid.

S: Does it get progressively harder, Vishrant, in the analogy of the onion, you know, as you're going deeper?

V: No, it depends what's there. It doesn't necessarily get progressively harder. It depends on what you've actually got there, what kind of traumas that you've actually repressed inside of you, held inside of you, and what level of pain body is attached to that. The problem with people who are victim-orientated, people who turn themselves into victims of situations and then run the story over and over again in their head, is whatever happened in the first place traumatised them and wounded them, and then every time they run it over in their head as a victim, they produce more energy, they produce more pain body. So, one of the things about healing the wounds the Heart is you've got to stop producing more. It's like you're in a boat that's got a hole in the bottom and that's you producing more by being a victim. The hole is letting water in and you're trying to bail it out, you're trying to heal it. Well, it doesn't work. You've got to stop being a victim and then you can bail it out by allowing yourself to feel what's there. It takes a fair bit because quite often we've got a fair bit inside. In our society, we're not programmed to express, we're programmed to repress. Most human adults have quite a large pain body and they do go through the dark night of the soul, if they're willing to feel it, if they're willing to open up or if something traumatises them and they get forced into it.

S: And are there various pain bodies? These are all new phrases, I'm sorry. I'm asking you to elaborate on some of them.

V: We just go into injustice wounding. "It's not fair." A lot of us were taught as children that there's such a thing as fairness and if we were programmed that way, when we get into the real world and it's actually not fair, we get all of this wounding because we don't think it's fair. It's injustice wounding, you know, and we repress these feelings about it not being fair and that gets stuck as a pain body.

So, there's just one type of pain body. In getting in touch with that, people think, "Oh, it's just pain". It's not just pain. When we get in touch with our wounding, there's helplessness and hopelessness attached inside of it, which is really yucky, because it makes us feel really bad. But if we're willing to feel it, it can go. It can pass. It can go and we can become sattvic. Most people you meet are rafting. They're sitting above their pain bodies, with a personality that lives probably projecting to the future. "Things will get better later." If we look at a lot of religions, that's what they sell. Things will get better later, heaven, and that's like an opiate that takes people away from what's inside of them now.

S: I hear you. Thank you.

V: Thank you.

~

S: Hi Vishrant. Vishrant, when something happens and I contract, my breath becomes very shallow. So should I work on my breath at that time, release it, or should I be looking at the belief system, whatever has made me contract?

V: Or you can do both. I used the breath extensively in training myself to let go because I know that if we breathe out fully, the mind can let go a lot easier. So I used the outward breath a lot to let go of things that my mind wasn't in agreement with and then I went and examined the belief systems that were supporting that non-agreement and I undid them because I wasn't interested in getting caught the same way. Needless to say, I failed heaps of times, but I kept going. I kept going. I kept undoing and undoing and undoing until things would happen that used to trigger me, used to contract me, but they no longer did, because the belief systems that supported that contraction weren't there anymore. They'd had enough doubt put into them to have lost their power.

I was just talking to Jyoti about injustice wounding. I had a fair bit of injustice wounding because I'd been brought up like everyone else thinking that life should be fair, and it took a while to for me to start really challenging that belief around fairness, that things should be fair, people should be fair. I finally saw right through it. It's like, no, look at the animal kingdom. Nothing's fair. The big animals eat the small animals, the old animals, the sick animals – that's what happens. There's no such thing as fairness. It's a mind-made understanding that's out of touch with reality. And we get into the human world, and of course, humans aren't fair either. They're just not. There's nothing wrong with you being fair because that's the Way of the Heart, to take care and to be fair, but expecting it to come from outside of you is really out of touch with the reality of the world we live in.

S: That's right. And thank you for this comparison or the insight of seeing the world itself – like there's no fairness in the world, the animal kingdom. It helps me a lot to understand this at a deeper level.

V: Yeah, but I'll say it again: there's nothing wrong with you being fair and you taking care of people, but expecting it outside of you is crazy because it's just not the way it is. Some people might be fair, some might not be fair. You don't know.

You know, we see people getting hurt in accidents. We see people getting sick with cancer or something else like that and we think "that's not fair". "They're so young or they're so innocent" or whatever, but it's just what is. There's no such thing as fairness.

S: And whenever someone behaves in an unfair way with us, for me, with me, then my mind goes like "I'm going to do the same to you, then you'll understand". So this is something I don't want to do, but it comes to my mind.

V: Yeah. Look, if someone's being unfair, if someone's being unjust, if someone's slandering you or libelling you in some way, they're just running true to their patterning. They're just running true. They can't help it. You know, if you were programmed that way, you might be that way as well. There but for the grace of God goes you. As a spiritual teacher, I'm telling the Truth worldwide constantly and I get a lot of slander, a lot of people saying things that aren't true, but it's just what is. What I discovered in this world is the darkness has to kill the light to survive. And it's okay. It's okay that it tries to do that. So what? It's just what is.

~

S: The next question has been written by Marcus. Why is formal meditation so important?

V: If you are present to reality, it's not. But if you went to school and learnt to live in your head, and now you live in your head, it's very important because formal meditation trains you to get out of your head and back into reality. It starts creating a default pattern of being with what is real, maybe your breath, rather than what you think, which is not real. Meditation is simply being aware of what is real. That is meditation. Formal meditation enables that. It's like reclaiming reality from the dream that you've been lost in because you got sent to school for so many years and learnt to live in your head. Formal meditation is good news, not bad news. It's wonderful stuff. It's about being present to reality. It's about programming the mind to start just being present to what is real, rather than to what you think.

S: The next question has been written by Diane: Wouldn't a past life just be a memory in the awake state and experience?

V: Yes, it would be. The initial memory of past life, I was curious. I was interested to see what would come of it and it expanded itself as years went by – more memory of how that person lived, the name of that person, what the person did, and how they felt about things. The next lot that came, I didn't want to know, but it just kept coming. The dream kept coming. The memory of life after life after life kept coming, lasted about a week-and-a-bit, and I didn't want it. I'd had enough, so I consciously stopped allowing it to come because I just didn't want it anymore. I'd seen enough. We get born over and over again. We die over and over again. And we suffer over and over again. We can get out of samsara by surrendering our life to Truth, by waking up.

~

S: Hi, Vishrant, my question was just that I feel like a lot of fear has developed from my last satori and I don't know how to deal with it.

V: Yeah, well, you're not okay with going crazy. You see, the two main fears that humans have are the fear of death and the fear of insanity, which is the fear of loss of control. Now, if you can be okay with the fear of death and you can be okay with the fear of insanity, you can get free. As long as you serve those fears, you will be stuck in the mind. I became willing to die and I also became willing to go insane. I became willing to let go of control basically, and put everything in God's hands. That's the only way. There is no other way. As long as you're hanging on to "I don't want to be insane" that attachment keeps you stuck. Very, very stuck. And it's supported by fear, which is not even real. It's a projection.

Look, in satori, you do lose your mind, but there's something inside of you that's not willing and it's holding you locked in the matrix of the mind. When satori occurs, the unknown presents itself, because the mind can't possibly know about Beingness because it doesn't have any reference points. The mind can't make any sense of it, so it throws up fear. Surrender. Allow whatever happens to happen. Give yourself to God. Give yourself to Truth. Let go, let go, let go.

S: Thank you. Okay.

~

S: The next question has been written by Brian: I have a profound love for Zen Buddhism, Sufism, and

Taoism. Are these attachments in the way of finding myself as Truth?

V: If you have a profound love of Zen, you'll understand that you have to let go of everything. Having a profound love and having a practice is very different. Zen is about nothing, nothing and nothing. Let go, let go, let go. There's nothing wrong with that. Now, understanding Zen, understanding Taoism, it's a whole different thing, isn't it, really? That's just collecting knowledge. Understanding Sufism, just collecting knowledge. The collection of knowledge doesn't make you more conscious, doesn't enlighten you. It just means you've collected knowledge. If you really love these things, practise what they teach, particularly Zen. Let go, let go, let go. Simplify, simplify, simplify. I also love Zen, but I practised Zen. That's up to you. What do you practise? Give up collecting knowledge and practise what's being taught. It's the practice that brings you home, not the intellectual understanding.

~

S: Hey Vishrant. How does Beingness connect with the material world in the form of being healthy because I know how important exercise is because exercise affects the mind a certain way? Can you talk about how doing things like exercise and staying healthy affects spiritual health?

V: Okay, so the body is a spacesuit and really, it's just a space suit. It's a biological spacesuit with an onboard computer. That's crazy enough, to think that it's you, but it's not you. It's just crazy. And the spacesuit is being powered by Beingness. Pure awareness. Now, if you don't take care of the space suit, it will deteriorate and die so it's good to take care of the spacesuit even though it's nothing to do with what you truly are or who you truly are. So, you take care of the spacesuit because the spacesuit's going to be used to visit this plane. As far as I'm concerned, that's about it. Wonderful spacesuit, take care of it, but that's up to you. If you don't take care of the spacesuit, well, suffer the consequences of the spacesuit getting sick and dying.

S: So like, it's gonna sound silly, but lately I've been thinking that eating not good all the time and not exercising at all is making it harder for me to get out of my head.

V: I see what you're saying. Yeah, look, my whole thing about getting out of my head was being present to reality, being present to what is real around me. Present moment awareness of what is real rather than present moment awareness of what is not real, which is what you think – that takes practice. Whether you're eating correctly or not eating correctly is not that relevant. What's relevant is where is your awareness at? Are you living in your head or is your awareness on what's real?

S: One more thing, which has been a big trauma of mine for my whole life. I would say the biggest one I'm aware of right now is a father wound because of, basically this is a sad story, but you know, it hits me where it hurts and I still don't feel that pain any less than I have, practising openness.

V: What pain's that?

S: It's the pain of having an absent father. Just hurts.

V: So, does that give you the feeling of not being loved?

S: Yeah, it makes me feel like an alien. Like no one understands.

V: So how old were you when your father left?

S: Like, four.

V: Okay. Okay, so you had an absent father, so that part's gone. What about you, championing your own inner child, which sounds like it could be wounded? Have you ever looked at inner child work?

S: I have, I just don't know how to do it.

V: Oh, it's pretty easy, really. You just use your imagination. You imagine that four-year-old boy, or you go back in your memory to that four-year-old. Imagine how that four-year-old boy was feeling at the time when dad left, and you go back as an adult, you go back and you champion that child and you say to that child, "I'm going to be with you from now on, you never need to be alone again". This is where it begins. And then you go back to every year to that child again, and there'll be something there, something will have happened, and you go back and you champion the child again, you tell that child you're there for them, you've got their back, you'll never leave them, you'll always be there for them. And what you're doing is developing a healthy relationship with the damage that's inside of yourself as a result of the absentee parent. You understand?

S: I understand.

V: But you have to do it. Thinking about it doesn't work, you have to do it, you have to go down and do it. I started doing this sometime in the 80s. I had a vision of a little boy underneath a table. And it was just a vision and I thought "That's odd," and then I looked closer, and I noticed that little boy was me when I was about two years old, crawling around on the floor under a table. And I went there and I just held the child and I just held it. That's all I did. I didn't know what else to do, but it just felt so nourishing to hold that child. And then I continued on and found all of those other children inside of myself at different ages that had been through different traumas and I went back as an adult and I was there for them, holding them, loving them, telling them I was going to be there for them. And in that way, I was starting to heal my own psyche. You understand?

S: Yeah. So it's a very intuitive process, you would say?

V: Well, I'd say it's intuitive, yeah, and it works, it works. But you've got to do it.

S: Right.

V: When I worked as a psychotherapist, I used hypnosis to take people back into their past, into their early childhood, right through their teenage years, looking at any trauma, any kind of pain body that might have been there, and having people go back and experience that child, love that child, offer the support to that child and also feel what was there – and in feeling it, healing it.

S: You know if you offered a course, I would definitely attend: official Vishrant guidance.

V: I don't work as a psychotherapist anymore. I haven't done for about 23 years. Yeah, not my cup of tea anymore. I just like having chats with people like yourself. Yeah, I've kind of gone beyond the mind.

S: Okay Vishrant, I'm gonna just imagine that young wounded Marcus and be there to love him. And all the details and stuff that will come intuitively, and just do it.

V: Well, that's best.

S: Got it, thank you.

V: Yeah, look if you go online, use Google and check out "championing the inner child," you will find a heap of information on it. It's quite a profound form of psychotherapy that I know works.

There's a guy called Bradshaw who put out a heap of tapes on the subject, videos on the subject. Very good. Very good stuff. Look up "Bradshaw championing the inner child" and you can find heaps of books that he put out, and heaps of tapes he put out, and he was on the money. He was very good at what he did.

S: Lovely.

V: Thank you for satsang. Good to see you bravehearts here today.

CHAPTER FOUR

How to Use Relationships for Higher Consciousness

V: I learned more about what's required for higher consciousness in relationship than probably in any other sphere because ultimately what we need to learn for Enlightenment and for higher consciousness and for awakening of the Heart is surrender. This is very difficult for us to learn because it's a non-doing. We learn surrender through the practice of acceptance, the practice of letting go, and when we're in relationship with another human being, we're always going to have differences. We're always going to have different opinions from time to time. There's always going to be a time when our partner is doing something that we don't agree with or saying something we don't agree with, and it's in those times that we can either practise resistance or practise surrender, practise being right or practise letting go.

Not everything goes as planned and can we accept the things that go wrong or the things that we don't agree with or are we going to get righteous and go into resistance and contraction? If we're willing to actually let go, we'll start to see the belief systems that come into play, that have expectations attached to them that when they're not met, we contract, and in seeing those belief systems, we can start to undo the belief systems that cause contractions, cause resistance in our lives.

A relationship with another human being can effectively be used to help raise your consciousness levels simply by not resisting, simply by accepting and seeing what the mind is up to, and undoing whatever obstacles are in the way. Anything that contracts us, anything that puts us in resistance you could clearly say is an obstacle towards higher consciousness, an obstacle towards Enlightenment, because the mind needs to be able to support what is found. When awareness finds itself, when Beingness finds itself, it needs to be supported in that. The mind doesn't want to be attracting attention back to itself, taking awareness away from awareness, awareness away from Beingness by going into massive contraction because it doesn't agree with the way the world is.

Developing an equanimous mind occurs as a result of the practise of acceptance and the seeing through of belief systems and undoing the ones that keep contracting you. This can commonly be called "the work" if you like or really just removing the obstacles that are in the way. But unless this work is done – unless the obstacles are removed – I don't feel Enlightenment is a possibility. If we have a mind that constantly contracts, awareness is going to go back to it, Beingness is going to go back to that mind, consciousness is going to go back to the mind and probably away from itself.

And so whatever relationship we're in, we can actually use that relationship to help us raise our consciousness levels by accepting instead of resisting.

If we fully accept anything, it's all over. The drama is over. The story is over. It's only when we're not in full acceptance that there is a continuance of something. So, it's really up to you. What are you going to do? How are you going to be in relationships? Are you going to be right? Are you going to be righteous? Are you going to be arrogant or are you going to be accepting? That doesn't mean that you don't communicate. It doesn't mean that you don't put a point across, but it does mean that you do it from a place of openness instead of a place of closure because the moment we're in resistance to our partner, we're closed. The moment we've contracted, we're closed.

If we want life to flow, we operate from a place of acceptance, and then life flows, no matter how hard life might be. If we're in a place of acceptance, life flows. The moment we contract, the moment we go into resistance, life becomes a little stuck for us because we're caught in our own minds in right, wrong, good, bad, and of course there are no bridges being built in that either. In practising acceptance, we're quite willing to build bridges to make it work. In practising resistance or "I'm right," you're wrong, we're not in bridge-building mode. We're actually in bridge-burning mode and that's destructive to relationships.

The practise of acceptance inside relationship supports the relationship. It also supports higher consciousness and that's up to you. If all you can do is be right, you're probably going to ruin your relationship. Acceptance is the oil that makes it work smoothly, and once again, it doesn't necessarily mean that you're closing down communication and allowing people to walk all over you. That's not what I'm talking about. I'm just talking about approaching life within relationship with another from a place of openness rather than a place of closure.

S: What is the importance of relationship between a spiritual teacher and disciple?

V: My relationships with my spiritual teachers were love affairs – love affairs in that I loved them completely, and in that love, I followed their instruction, and in that love, they passed something to me. In that love, there was the transmission of the lamp, the transmission of Beingness, so what is here, what is aware here could become aware of itself, and that was done in a love affair, a love affair with Truth because the master is Truth. The master might look like a person, but they are no longer a person. They are Truth. They're knowing themselves as Beingness. It's just Truth. The person has gone, and so the disciple falls in love with Truth basically, and in that love affair, the disciple gives themselves 100 per cent to Truth. Another word for Truth is God. The disciple gives their life to God. So, anybody who has awoken has given their life to Truth or given their life to God. They don't keep their life anymore. It's over. This is also why they're free. That part that gave is now surrendered. There's an absence of that part now. Someone who's awake is existing as Beingness, not as an "I" any longer. It is over. And it is in that relationship between the disciple and the master that this can occur. It is the most beautiful thing where the disciple gives their life to Truth, gives their life to God in that love affair because love is the most beautiful thing. It's the only thing that is valuable here. Nothing else has value but love. It is in that love affair that the mind prepares to unconditionally surrender, which is like a death to Truth, to Beingness, to God, whatever you want to call it. But it's an end.

~

S: What do you mean when you speak about the need for the seeker to stand alone and how does this occur in relationship?

V: Okay. The world we live in is not that conscious and when you start going for higher consciousness and you start achieving it, you're highly unlikely to be supported by it because we're not living in monasteries or ashrams. The people I talk to are lay people who have families, who have jobs in the marketplace, and it's highly unlikely they're going to get supported in their spiritual quest by the people who they work with, by the people who are related to them or by the people they live with because they're not into it and they don't understand it. They think you're a little bit strange. So you have to be able to stand alone in surrender, and that's difficult, but it's a requirement.

You can't be pulled here and there and everywhere away from Truth if you're into it. You actually have to put Truth first and you have to be able to stand alone in surrender – "alone" meaning not supported. If you're with a spiritual teacher or a master, you're with someone who will support you in that awakening, in that quest, and if you're with a community of people who are into it, a sangha, they will support you in that quest as well. If you're with a partner who will support you, that is optimal.

If you're not with a partner who can support you, it is difficult. It is difficult. There is no doubt about that, but that goes for anything in life really, in business, in music and in an art. If you're with someone who's not supporting what you're doing, it's difficult. It's not impossible, but you still do need to be able to learn to stand alone in surrender so you don't get pulled away. And so, you keep Truth as number one.

~

S: Do you think it's a problem if my partner is not interested in Truth and Enlightenment as much as I am?

V: It can be a problem, but it can be handled depending on how your partner handles your interest. Sometimes a partner who's not into Truth will support the other partner who is into Truth and sometimes they won't, and if they won't, that becomes very difficult. It can be a reason for conflict or argument. It's always best to be with people who are going in the same direction as yourself. There's no doubt about that, in whatever endeavour you're doing in life. It can get very, very difficult if you're with someone who's not into Truth, particularly if you decide to put Truth first – and the seeker who finds themselves as Truth, the seeker who wakes up, always, always, always puts Truth first.

~

S: My partner betrayed me and I feel empty inside. How do I find my joy again?

V: Accept the betrayal. I have been betrayed so many times and what I learned is that human beings betray. Whether it's our partners or friends or children or business deals we do, it's human nature to betray and it is our being out of touch with reality to think that it should be different. I accept betrayal because it is what it is. It's there. It's unrealistic of me to think that it shouldn't be there because it is there.

Everybody has these weaknesses. You yourself have betrayed, and if you haven't, that's highly unlikely. Every time we have a pornographic thought about someone besides our partner, in a way we've betrayed. It is okay. Make it okay or suffer. Your choice. If you can't accept what is, you will suffer. If you can accept what is, suffering ends. Acceptance is the answer. And there isn't another one. That's it. And that's in your hands because you're the one who can accept or not, regardless of what the other is doing. You're the one creating your suffering because of your resistance to what is.

~

S: Do you think that having kids can be an obstacle to being a seeker of Truth?

V: Heck no, more opportunities for surrender. I had three children and I didn't see them as obstacles at all. Of course, they needed attention and they needed my awareness with them a lot. I still had my spiritual practices of meditation, self-inquiry, and openness, and they didn't interfere with any of those because

I was involved in meditation and self-inquiry when they were asleep or they were at school or early in the morning before they got up. And with the practice of openness, well, having kids is wonderful for the practice of openness because kids get into all sorts of things they shouldn't and you can be open with them and still put the boundaries in place. You do not have to contract. You do not have to go into resistance. It's another way of learning how to be accepting through the practice of acceptance. Up to you.

~

S: Putting Truth first before my partner and my kids seems a bit selfish at times. What is your take on that?

V: Putting Truth first, okay. Here's the take. If you wake up, would that be good for your kids and your partner or not? You see, to wake up, you have to sacrifice your life for Truth because you surrender unconditionally to Truth. You don't get to keep anything. You surrender unconditionally to Truth and then you become a light for those who want to see in the darkness – including your partner, including your children. So, which is best for them really? Which is best for your children, really? Oh, on that note, there's no such thing as selfish Enlightenment. That's not a possibility. The self that you know as you doesn't make it to Enlightenment. The self that you know as you sacrifices itself, surrenders itself unconditionally. So, it's not selfish to wake up. It's a completely unselfish act.

~

S: Often I find myself looking at my relationship to make me feel complete. Is this possible?

V: I've heard the statement "you complete me," which might make you feel good about you. You want to be complete. You want to be whole? Accept yourself totally as you are and love yourself. Then you become self-nourishing which has nothing to do with anything outside of you. As a matter of fact, if you are not self-nourishing – if you're a beggar looking for love outside of you – you're always going to be looking for love outside of you, you're always going to be in problems. The best thing you can do for you is find a way to accept you and love you as you are. Then when you meet someone, you can love them because you're not coming in as a beggar, you're coming in with love. You're coming in with something to give, rather than something to take.

So, when we say someone completes us, it means there's something missing in us and that missing would be self-nourishing. When we're self-nourishing, love starts to overflow in us and then we can share that love, and that is giving and that is very beautiful. That means as a psyche, we've actually self-accepted completely. Have a look. Have a look and see if you're self-nourishing or if it is that you need something from someone else to make you feel nourished. Because when two people come together who are both self-nourishing, wow, they just bring love in. They're just two givers coming together rather than two beggars or a beggar and a giver coming together. It all begins with self-acceptance. How are you inside of yourself with you? How loving are you with you? Because if you're loving with you, you're self-nourishing and then that gets shared. Then you're a giver rather than a beggar.

~

S: When there are difficult things to express within a relationship, is the first step to accept the situation as it is?'

V: The first step is to accept the other. You know, when we have difficult times in relationships, we quite often take our own side, and in that way, it becomes a bit of a war. If you really want good communication with anybody, make sure that you're not only on your own side, you're also on their side; and if you're on their side, you'll be able to put yourself in their shoes and you'll be able to hear them from their point of view, which actually facilitates communication.

Acceptance plays a big role in it. There's no doubt about it. But so does communication. When we truly look at what keeps relationships going in a healthy way, first is communication, second is commitment – those two things, commitment and communication. But when we're only taking our own side, inside of a disagreement in an argument, we've basically gone to war, and unfortunately the first casualty of war is usually truth. And this appears in the form of omission. Things aren't said that should be said. Things aren't owned that should be owned. So, you have a look. Acceptance is great. Accepting the other is wonderful. Accepting everything as it is is wonderful, but if you want relationships to work well, particularly if you're in disagreements, make sure that you're on both sides – your side and their side.

~

S: After being in a relationship for many years, I find that it feels quite stale.

How can I bring present moment awareness into my relationship to liven it up?

V: If your relationship feels quite stale, it is because there is no present moment awareness in the relationship because if you are present to reality in the moment, everything is fresh, always fresh. It is only when we are living in our heads that everything becomes stale and seemingly repetitive which is actually not a possibility because everything that happens is new, every moment. And so, you asked me about present moment awareness. It sounds like there's a lack of present moment awareness in your relationship. It sounds like you're actually just projecting constantly on to the other and thinking that somehow the same thing is happening over and over again which is actually not possible. Every moment is fresh. If you truly come into the moment, everybody is new every moment, but if you're living in your head projecting, that's not the case. You get bored because you're just projecting the same thing over and over again, thinking there's some kind of repetition, which in fact there is not because there can't be. Every moment is new. Every moment is fresh. This is the "Power of Now."

~

S: Sometimes when my partner chews loudly while eating, I find it very irritating. Where do I start if I want to accept the things that I don't like about my partner?

V: Yeah, look, I used to be quite trippy when I was younger and I found that just going to the cinema and someone was eating chips close to me, it would irritate me and take my awareness away from what was on the big screen. Grrr. What I learned was that if I had a look inside of myself and had a look at what belief systems were in play, I could start to undo them, and I found that in undoing belief systems inside of myself about the things that got me, those things no longer got me. And so, I undid all of the belief systems that I could find inside of myself and I found that things that used to trip me up, no longer tripped me up, because I'd undone me. I hadn't tried to change outside of me. I hadn't stood up in the theatre and turned around and said "Stop chewing crisps!" I'd undone the belief systems inside of myself that they shouldn't be chewing chips and they shouldn't be chewing them loudly. I made it okay. And in that making it okay, I became free of those trips. It's up to you. It's your trip, not the person who is chewing loudly. You're the one who has a problem. You're the one who can solve it inside of you. Not outside of you. Make it okay. Be okay with it. Undo any belief systems that it's not okay and be free. Your choice.

~

S: When my wife looks at other men passing by when we are out together, I feel jealousy and rage. How can

I stop this as it's very destructive to my relationship and creates a lot of problems?

V: Yeah, right? Jealousy is a very destructive process. I got in touch with jealousy when I was very young and realised how dangerous it was and so I decided not to support jealousy in any way, shape or form inside of myself because it's so destructive. People kill each other over it and it's going to be really, really up to you, because you can't control your wife from looking at other men if she wants to. That's her prerogative, her right. It's not like she's doing anything wrong. The trip is in you. You've got a problem and you're creating that problem with your belief systems. You're creating that problem with your jealousy.

How about accepting that your wife likes to look at other men? What's so wrong with that? Except in your mind, you know, it's up to you. What's going on with you? It will be very destructive and destroy your relationship. Your choice, and then do it to the next one as well because it doesn't stop. Jealousy is so destructive and you're responsible for your jealousy.

How about just accepting that your wife likes to look at other men? Stop blaming her, because you wouldn't be enraged unless you are blaming. You're doing the blaming, not her. You're putting the effort into blaming not her. You're becoming a victim of her looking. You're doing that. You're responsible 100 per cent for your feelings and what you're doing in your mind, not her. I'll leave you with that.

~

S: I like being in a relationship, but I also want to dedicate my time to Truth. How do I balance my romantic relationship with my dedication to Truth?
V: Put Truth first. If you're a seeker, you put Truth first and the relationship is there and you give the relationship what it needs to work as well, but you put Truth first. You see, there's nothing worth doing on this plane except waking up. Everything else is wasting time. Put all effort into waking up and you can be in relationship and you can love your partner and you can take care of them and you can practise openness with them and you can practise acceptance with them. You can practise all of the things that you need to practise for higher consciousness with them, but put Truth first. Waking up is more important than anything else on this plane. Nothing else is more important than waking up. Become a light so others can see. This planet is in darkness. It is in chaos and it is in a destructive mode. The only thing that is going to save it now is higher consciousness and that's up to you, not someone else, and higher consciousness occurs when we wake up, when awareness becomes aware of itself, when we know ourselves as Beingness, and then we are a light in the darkness for those who cannot see yet.

~

S: I find I have a higher sex drive than my wife. How can I let go of that desire and find contentment without it?
V: Okay, you have to accept what is or suffer incredibly. Your choice. You have a greater sex drive than

your wife. So what? That's what it is. You can either make it a problem or you can accept it as it is. Your choice. Really your choice. If you don't accept it as it is, you're going to suffer. You're going to turn yourself into a victim of your wife's lower sex drive and then you'll probably try and hurt her because you'll get bitter and resentful, but all because of your own story, not because of reality. Just because someone has a lower sex drive than you doesn't mean that they're any less than you or any more than you. Acceptance is the answer. Up to you. Accept or suffer.

~

S: How do I not get attached to my relationship?
V: It is almost impossible for a human being not to get attached inside of a relationship because it's chemical bonding. Some people say "Ooh, I have love at first sight". No, you do not have love at first sight, you have chemical bonding at first sight. That's where a whole pile of chemistry goes off inside of you and blinds you to the obvious faults of the other so you can have sex, have babies, and keep the survival of the species going. People love to call it love, but really it is just hormones. It's just chemical fireworks, if you like, and after a certain period of time, that wears off. Then you start to see the person who you're with, what they're really like, rather than through these hormone-fuelled eyes, and then you have to decide whether you're going to stay with them or not, once you've seen the obvious faults, which for some reason or another you didn't see before because of being blinded by hormones.

So, everybody gets attached in relationships because of this primal bonding that occurs. If you don't want to be attached in a relationship, wake up, and then you're not attached to anything. It's over.

~

S: How would you teach your kids about higher consciousness?

V: Very simple. Gain higher consciousness. Kids copy you, so if you have higher consciousness and your kids are hanging out with you, they're going to see higher consciousness. They're going to see the role of how higher consciousness works in the world. Children live by and learn by copying their parents. If all you do is wallow around in lower consciousness, that's all you're teaching your children. If you start operating from higher consciousness, you're teaching them another way to be in the world. You have become their best teachers. That's up to you. Whatever sins the parents have, they do pass to the children one way or another. If you really want your children to have higher consciousness, gain it and live it yourself.

~

S: Do you think it's easier to wake up if you're celibate to avoid distractions from the quest for Truth?

V: Maybe. I don't know. I never became a monk. I never took celibacy vows. I don't know. I do know that what's required for awakening is unconditional surrender. Sexuality plays no part in that. If you can practise acceptance inside of a relationship with a woman or a man, you're actually practising what will take you to higher consciousness. You're preparing the mind for Enlightenment. Now, if you don't have a relationship with a man or a woman, there are other things to surrender to so both ways work. I don't see a huge advantage in either way because if a person is willing to surrender, willing to accept their partner or whatever their life circumstances, they are preparing the mind for Enlightenment. I do not believe we need to be celibate to become enlightened, because that's just not the case. That's just not true.

Whether it's an advantage to be celibate or not, I really don't know. Not my experience. I know that inside of relationship, we have every opportunity to learn what we need to learn to raise our consciousness levels because we have something we can accept. We have something that is going to be different than what we want from time to time and give us opportunities to practise acceptance and surrender. Up to you.

~

S: I find myself fluctuating between the path of spirituality and wanting the relationship to go well. Are these paths mutually exclusive?

V: No, not at all. If you want your relationship to go well, practise building bridges inside of the relationship rather than burning them, and to build bridges inside any relationship we have to practise acceptance of the other. In practising acceptance of the other, we are doing what's required to raise our consciousness levels. So, they can work hand in hand. They don't have to be against each other at all. A relationship can absolutely aid in raising consciousness levels if you're willing to use it that way, but if all you're going to do in relationship is want to be right, want to be arrogant, you're just going to destroy the relationship and end up with a relationship probably based on a business deal regarding land and children rather than a relationship based on love. When we bring acceptance into our relationships, love can flourish. When there is no acceptance, when there is just resistance, there is no love, there's just business deals. So, I see them as working hand in hand, particularly if you're practising acceptance.

S: Is it true, I can only really be in a relationship once I learn to be alone?

V: No, you can be in a relationship anytime. As a matter of fact, you're in a relationship when you're born, with your mother, probably your father and maybe siblings and the dog and the cat. We're very social, social beings, human beings. We're in relationship most of our lives one way or another, whether that's in business or personal relationship, or even just a relationship with the girl down at the petrol station when we say hello and goodbye. We're very social beings.

Being alone helps in this. If you can actually be alone and be happy, you're not going to have too many problems inside of a relationship because you're not coming in as a beggar, as someone who needs someone else to make themselves feel happy. So, it's not a bad idea for you to spend some time alone before you get into relationship to see how you are with you, to see if you can be alone without this constant neediness for someone else to fulfill those needs, being self-sufficient, self-contained. Then when you come into relationship, you actually have something to give rather than something that you want to take. So, there's nothing wrong with spending time alone, but you don't necessarily need to. Relationships work because people come in as givers. If you're in a relationship, find your Heart and become a giver because when you do find your Heart, all you're going to want to do is give. It's very beautiful. If all you're doing is coming into relationship needing the other's support, needing the other's love, you've come in as a beggar. And if they've come in the same way, well, you have two beggars together and you basically have a loveless relationship. Being alone allows us to find a way to be with ourselves, to be self-accepting, to be self-nourishing. Then we have a gift because that nourishment will flow on to the other. So, it's an advantage to be able to be alone, but it's not necessary. It's up to you. You're going to create your reality, nobody else.

~

S: I find at times I have an addictive demand for my partner to be a certain way. How can I let go of that attachment and be okay with things just as they are?
V: Don't let it go. Hang on to the attachment and then it won't be too long before you'll need a new relationship because you'll destroy the one you're in. Anytime we addictively demand anything we become unreasonable. Anytime we addictively demand anything, we're in resistance to life and we're out of

touch with our hearts. If you want your relationship to work, find a way to be open – and there's no room for addictive demands in openness. If you find that you can be open, you can find love, and in love, you just want to serve the other because that's the beauty of love. That's how it affects the mind. You just want to take care of everyone and everything. That's the Way of the Heart. That's the Beauty Way. That's the best way to live on this planet, the Way of the Heart. But it does demand that you be open because in openness, love is perceived. In closure, it's barely noticed, if at all. When you're addictively demanding anything you're too closed. That's just that.

Thank you for satsang. Good to see you bravehearts here today.

CHAPTER FIVE

Overcoming Suffering

V: Welcome to satsang.
S: Good morning.
V: Good morning.
S: Could you speak about overcoming suffering?
V: Okay.

Well, the Buddha stated that life is dissatisfying in the first of the Four Noble Truths and it's absolutely true. Life is dissatisfying. And the reason for that is very simple: we're constantly desiring things to be different than how they are.

Now, a mild desire doesn't create suffering. But a strong desire does, because it's a form of resistance. So how can we have a life where we don't suffer? Well, simple: don't resist. But that's more difficult than meets the eye because we're programmed to resist. We're programmed actually to contract. We're programmed to that, to actually suffer.

The other thing that causes suffering is when we get attached to something and then it gets threatened or we fear that it's going to be in some way damaged or taken away. We then go into resistance again. So once again, resistance causes suffering.

The two major things that cause suffering, desires, and attachments, which is what the Buddha stated in the second of the Four Noble Truths, is absolutely true. He got it right 2500 years ago. This is what causes suffering. Most people don't really get it. They don't get that they are creating their own suffering by the resistance they're putting into what they want or what they're trying to protect. At some point, in consciousness rising, you get to see, "Aha! If I don't resist, if I don't contract to life, I'm not going to suffer anywhere near as much as I have been". And that's absolutely true. Profoundly correct. But it's difficult, because we probably got that information later in life, after the age of seven. And after the age of seven, we've all got default patterns of resistance and contraction, probably based around belief systems that have expectations on them, and when those expectations aren't met, there's contraction and resistance, and so in that way we've been programmed to suffer. But as adults, we can change that. As adults, we can see it and stop resisting, stop contracting to life. I teach the Way of the Heart and for me the Way of the Heart is the practise of openness. When we're wide open, we feel love, and when we feel love, we want to take care of everything and everyone, which is very beautiful. It's a beautiful way to live.

But in openness, there's no contraction, there's no resistance, and so there's no suffering. There may still be pain, but pain is not suffering. Pain is pain. Suffering is when we resist pain. The less you can resist life, the less you suffer. I watch people get offended by things and that's them deciding to suffer, not consciously, but that's exactly what's happening. The moment we take offence, we go into resistance to what is. We suffer, and we suffer at our own hands – though most people wouldn't like to take responsibility for that. They'd prefer to blame something else for that. That is immaturity. Blaming someone else or something else for how you feel – considering you're the one who makes you feel – is immature. In a lot of ways that comes back to maturity levels. How willing are you to take responsibility for your life? How willing are you to take responsibility for your feelings? Because you make you feel. The world and other people cannot make you feel. Only you can do that. The world can do things you don't like. People can do things you don't like. But you're the one who makes you feel. You create the resistance or the non-resistance. In other words, you create your suffering. And this is how we create our reality, by the way we think about the world through our reactions.

So how not to suffer? Stop resisting life. Learn to be open. Learn to accept life. That doesn't make you ineffective. You can still change things from acceptance, from openness. It just means you don't suffer while you're doing it. Now, when we look at this from a perspective of intelligence, it is not smart to create suffering for yourself. See the point? Stop suffering. Stop resisting life. See the point. Whatever you practise, you're going to get good at. Stop resisting life. Start accepting it and watch how the suffering disappears. It's going to be up to you because only you can do this. Nobody can do it for you.

Are there any questions, any statements or any challenges to this teaching here today?

S: The first question. Willingness is required for higher consciousness. Is there anything we can do to train willingness in ourselves?

V: Well, if you're not willing, you're not willing. I had one teacher, his name was Teertha. He used to say, "Well, you just haven't suffered enough yet". I don't know if that's true or not, but there is something in it. It's like, if you're not willing, why aren't you willing? Only you can answer that question. Nobody can answer that question for you. If you're not willing, maybe it's because you have blinded yourself to what's going on. Maybe you're living in hope that things are going to get better or someone's going to wave a magic wand over you and it's all going to be okay. Take off your blinkers. Take off your rose-coloured glasses and have a look. You create your reality and if you're not willing to change it so you don't suffer, wow, you must not be seeing something.

S: Is openness the only thing we are required to do to nullify resistance?

V: You can't be in resistance and be open. It's that simple. Openness is wonderful because you can practise it and nobody knows you're practising it. People can be having an argument with you and you're practising openness. In other words, you're practising non-resistance and non-contraction. Nobody needs to know. And you know, people talk about, "I haven't got time for a spiritual practice". How about practising openness in the marketplace? You've got time for it. Nobody knows you're doing it. And it'll show you where all of the obstacles inside of you are for your freedom. Because in the practise of openness, you get to see what contracts you. You get to see what needs to be undone. You get to see how you resist. You get to see the very things that stop you from perceiving your own Heart. Openness is brilliant. It counts for everything.

S: Do I have to suffer long enough before I can truly surrender?

V: You don't have to suffer at all. But if you want to, well nobody's gonna stop you. Do you have to suffer long enough? That's ridiculous. It's up to you. You're gonna create your reality. If you want to suffer, you just go ahead and suffer and see if it makes a difference. It doesn't change anything.

You know, I watch these people go into protest against all sorts of different things. And they go in angry, in resistance, and they create much suffering for themselves – which, by the way, they share with everybody they're with. And they think that somehow they're making a difference on the planet. What they bring is more darkness to the planet. You can go into a protest from openness and put your hand up and say "I don't like this". You can stand in front of a tree that's going to be cut down in a place of openness. You don't have to be angry. You don't have to be in resistance. You don't have to be suffering yourself. But people don't understand that. It's like, gosh, you want more light on the planet? Find love. And love happens as a result of openness, not as a result of contraction and resistance because you think someone's doing something wrong. Stop suffering. It doesn't change a thing.

S: I feel upset with my partner. It feels like a negative filter is over all aspects of my life.

V: You feel upset when you feel upset with your partner. It feels like a negative filter is over all aspects of my life. How can I escape? This is a wonderful old saying. This is from a husband's perspective anyway: happy wife, happy life.

We care about the people we love. We care about our partners, and when they're not happy or when we're not happy with them, it affects everything. But we don't have to rely on them for our happiness. We can be happy independently of how they are feeling or how they are doing or what's happening inside of them. But that would mean that we'd have to be self-contained and self-loving, rather than reliant on an outside source for our happiness. And when we look at higher consciousness, in a lot of ways, it is about being self-contained, being self-loving, self-accepting and self-nurturing. And we're only talking to the perspective of the ego right now and the mind. But a mind that is self-nurturing can rest. A mind that is not self-nurturing is constantly looking for nurturing outside itself. It's affected quite strongly by what happens outside itself. And you say you're upset with your partner. Oh, dear. The world is never ever going to agree with everything we want. Being upset is a choice. You don't have to be upset.

You can make it okay. You don't have to be in the relationship if you don't want to. You can create communication if you want to change things, but being upset, is that some form of you trying to manipulate your environment? I don't know. Have a look for yourself. There's no point. You're just creating suffering for what? What does that change? I don't see any point in suffering. I don't see any point in resisting life. There's just no need for it. You have to volunteer to do it. Life is the way it is. Things aren't going to go the way we want all of the time. We don't have to suffer as a result of that. We can accept life as it is. But of course, that's up to us. It's much easier to do that if we are self-nurturing, if we have self-acceptance and self-love, because we're more self-contained. We're not reliant on trying to get love outside of ourselves or acceptance outside of ourselves. The foundation for higher consciousness is self-acceptance and that's completely up to you because no one can help you with that but you. So you're asking how can you escape feelings? Stop creating them. You're responsible. It's nobody else. Nobody else is doing anything to you. You're doing it to yourself. How can you escape? Stop it. Accept things as they are. Use communication to make things work if you want to or leave if you want to. But there's no point suffering. Okay?

S: Did you always choose to surrender in your romantic relationships? Did you sometimes decide it was better to give the relationship up?

V: Romantic relationships? Wow, that's an interesting term. I don't think I'm a romantic type. Actually, I'm too pragmatic. I don't mind buying flowers and getting a beautiful card sometimes and maybe writing some poetry, but I've never seen myself as a romantic type. More pragmatic. If I love someone, I let them know.

I don't think I've ever been asked that question before. Can you repeat the question for me? I got caught on the romantic bit.

S: Did you always choose to surrender in your romantic relationships or did you sometimes decide it was better to give the relationship up?

V: I've never been one to give up relationships. I've more or less been the guy who tries to make them work, rather than give them up.

I had a couple of rules involved in personal relationships. And those rules were no abandonment, no threat of abandonment, and no anger. And the reason that I had these rules was I could see clearly that I didn't want to manipulate and control someone through their wounding because most humans have abandonment wounding. I saw that as cruelty. I saw anger as a form of violence and I didn't want to be violent with my partner or anyone else for that matter. A lot of people don't see anger as violence, but I actually do see anger as violence. We're injecting someone with toxic energy when we're angry with them.

They're the two rules that I had. This idea of surrendering? I'm more accepting than anything else. Everybody's different. Nobody's going to agree with everything you have to say no matter who they are. People from the same family have differences, different understandings. I found that acceptance is the key to making relationships work. You have to accept the other – the good, the bad, and the ugly of the other – and keep communication open. That works. Relationships are difficult to navigate because you've got two people who want to control their environments together and they have different understandings of how to do that. It's always a little difficult and sometimes it's very, very difficult. Maybe you do need to leave the relationship because it's too destructive, but I've never been one to leave relationship. I've been one to try to build bridges and make it work.

I remember one of my teachers, Osho Rajneesh, talked about relationships. He said, "It doesn't matter what woman you get together with, learn to surrender, learn to accept, and then you can use the relationship for higher consciousness". And I heard that. I heard that clearly. So every relationship I've been in since the early 80s has been an opportunity to practise acceptance and surrender. It's the people who are close to us who can show us where we're still stuck inside ourselves, where we haven't shown up with love, where we're still in resistance. So, no abandoning.

S: A viewer on Facebook has asked: I am really struggling being with people close to me when they are stoned or intoxicated. How do I manage this?

V: Yeah, it is difficult because when people get stoned and intoxicated, they go into lower consciousness. They don't go into higher consciousness. And so it's difficult to be with them and communicate with them, and some of them may have bad habits in those spaces as well. I operate from a place of acceptance.

I accept people wherever they're at, but I don't live with people who get stoned or get intoxicated. It's not one of the things that I'm involved in. I'm involved in higher consciousness, and I don't really get involved in lower consciousness at all.

And once upon a time, a long time ago, yeah, that could have been me. So there but for the grace of God goes I. But I saw the light and I saw that that basically is just a form of escapism. People medicate themselves to make themselves feel better because life is hard. It's hard for every human being. And I've always seen people who actually aren't into higher consciousness – if they're medicating themselves on legal or illegal drugs, or alcohol is a drug as well – it's like, it's okay. It's okay that they do that. I don't have a problem with it. If they're into higher consciousness though, it's the wrong way. It just takes you back into lower consciousness. It darkens you. It doesn't make you brighter. It doesn't give you more clarity.

They say there's certain drugs that will give you insights like ayahuasca. Insights are only invitations to do the work. They're not the answer. Other drugs can relax you. Fair enough. But if you're really into higher consciousness, you don't really want to get involved in mind-altering substances. It's up to you. I'm not laying down any rules. Whatever people do is their business, but if you're into higher consciousness, you need clarity. Not unconsciousness, not dream. Most drugs take you into dream and dream is lower consciousness. If you're into higher consciousness, you need sanctuary, and it's difficult if you're with people who are doing a lot of alcohol or a lot of drugs. It may mean that you need to find somewhere else to live. I don't know your whole situation. But here's the thing about higher consciousness: it's always best to be with people going in the same direction, whatever that direction may be. If you want to get to the end, get to the goal. People who are into higher consciousness tend to hang out with people who are into higher consciousness. People who are into lower consciousness tend to hang out with people who are in lower consciousness. Birds of a feather flock together.

I've left behind many groups in my life for different reasons. And some of those groups, who were involved in alcohol and drugs, because I'd left that scene, I didn't want to know about it anymore. I didn't want to listen to someone talking to me from a stoned place about rubbish. Maybe if I was stoned, it would sound really interesting and reasonable, but when you're not stoned and when you have clarity it just sounds like rubbish. So, it's difficult. It's going to be up to you. What are you going to do? There could be some hard choices here for you. If you're into higher consciousness, it's always best to hang out with people who enjoy higher consciousness, always. Oh, and people who do drugs really, truly, are they into higher consciousness or are they just escaping something? Have a look.

~

S: Good morning, Vishrant. That question just triggered a memory in me that I remember Osho being asked in discourse one time: "Osho, can you tell us what do you think about drugs? Are they okay?" And he said this was an interesting question. If you are the master, then it is okay. If the drugs are the master, then it is definitely not okay. And that sort of resonated with me.

V: Yeah, he's talking about addiction.

S: Yeah, exactly. I mean, because I took drugs as probably all of us did. I took recreational drugs in my time. Hadn't for quite a long time, but . . . I just had to say that just triggered a memory, so I thought I'd share it.

V: Yeah, I've heard what Osho had to say on drugs as well and I had to have a really good look at myself at some point when I was using marijuana and I realised that really I was just trying to get away from something. I was just relaxing my mind because it had been basically disturbed by the day or whatever. So I was trying to take the edge off that. But what I realised is it just lowered my consciousness levels. It didn't give me more clarity. It didn't raise my consciousness levels. It just took me down. And I was really into higher consciousness. I was a seeker. So I just had to give it all away.

What are you into? You know, basically it comes back to what are you into? Are you into escaping or are you into higher consciousness?

S: Yeah, I totally agree. If you're into higher consciousness, and you don't need that stuff, and it's actually a stumbling block . . . anyway, thanks for that.

~

S: This question comes from a viewer: Sometimes I experience prolonged, ongoing pain and it feels like suffering. How do I differentiate between the two or change my point of view about the pain?
V: Okay.

Prolonged pain is chronic pain. Yeah. See, I have one answer and I don't have a second answer. The answer is acceptance. The pain doesn't go away because we accept, but the suffering does. The suffering that we have is created by our resistance to pain. Pain is just pain. In acceptance, the pain doesn't go away, but the suffering does. It's up to you. It's hard for us to learn acceptance because it's not part of our programming, our primal programming, but it is possible. In my life, I've accepted pain because I've been involved in basically a lot of sports that were painful so I actually found ways to accept pain, and in learning to accept pain, the suffering left, but the pain sometimes didn't.

So I only have one answer, and that's acceptance. But also, you know, if you can find medications that will take the pain away, if it's physical pain, there's nothing wrong with that. That's up to you too.

I teach acceptance, because it is the answer to freedom. And there actually isn't another one.

~

S: Do you think that psychotherapy can help someone to suffer less?
V: Heck yeah. It could also help someone suffer more, depending on what happens inside the psychotherapy process. We get involved in psychotherapy and

suddenly we become our own psychotherapists. We become our own analysts, and people can think that somehow that is going to help us spiritually grow. But the truth is, now we have another program where we're problem solving inside of our own mind. And then we're caught in our own minds again, psychoanalysing ourselves, and this happens to a lot of seekers. Actually, they get caught in psychoanalysing themselves and think that somehow they're raising their consciousness levels when the truth is they're dreaming. Because if you're analysing yourself, you're dreaming, and it becomes a pattern because we've all been programmed at school to see problems and solve them. That's what we're taught at school. In psychoanalysis, we can actually put that programming into play, thinking that somehow we're doing ourselves an amazing amount of good when really, we're just taking ourselves into another dream where we hurt ourselves. So there's a danger in it.

What's best is developing a silent witness that just watches the mind and then we settle. No need to analyse. No need to work it out. No need to rationalise. We just see it. And because it's seen, it can be stopped. Until we see what our minds are up to, there's nothing we can do about it. It just runs automatically and unconsciously. In witnessing the mind, we then get choices – to continue what we're doing, which is probably reaction, or to respond. Witnessing the mind, developing a silent witness is probably the best thing a human being can do towards higher consciousness.

S: If those that we love become destructive in their substance abuse, is it okay to completely remove them from our lives? Or is this unsupportive?

V: Depends on what you mean by destructive. It's a very hard question to answer because I don't know the circumstances. I don't know the situation.

S: Okay, the next question. It has been shown that mindfulness training helps people manage physical pain too. What is your understanding of how this works?

V: Well, wherever we put it, our awareness, we live. It's very simple. If you put your awareness on pain, you live as pain. We go through different processes during the day. If we're sad for some reason, and we put our awareness on sadness, we live as sadness. If we're angry and we put our awareness on anger, we live as anger. If we have pain, we put our awareness there, we live as pain. Wherever we put our awareness, we live. That's the same for people who are awake. Awareness is on awareness, then a person basically lives as Beingness. It's a little bit hard to say. Awareness on awareness is just awake. Awareness on anything is where we live though. If you put all of your awareness on the pain, of course you're going to be in pain.

So, if we put awareness on an ambient awareness, mindful of everything around us at once, then we're not focused on one thing, the pain will seem like it's less. We put all our awareness on the pain, it'll seem like it's more because it's our total focus.

Mindfulness training, being mindful of what is real ... the pain is real, by the way, but other things are real as well. Your breath is real. What you see is real. What you hear is real. What you're feeling is real. So if we have an ambient awareness or mindfulness of other things besides the pain, it does lessen the experience of the pain because we have our awareness spread. But if we have our awareness just totally on the pain, then that's what we pick up: pain. It becomes our totality. So yes, mindfulness training definitely helps deal with pain.

~

S: Is the ego addicted to suffering?
V: I don't think you can say that the ego is addicted to suffering. I can say, you can say, that people are unconscious, and they don't know what they're doing. If you're not aware that you're creating the suffering by what you're doing, well, you're ignorant. You actually haven't had a look. I don't think there's an addiction from the ego side to suffering. I think it's just ignorance that creates suffering in people because as your consciousness levels rise you get to see that you create that suffering.

So why would you want to do it? It's only out of ignorance that people suffer. If you watch the mind long enough, you'll see how it all works. You'll see how it creates whatever's going on, pretty much. But if you watch the mind long enough, you also get to see that you don't actually have to resist life. You don't have to create that suffering. That's up to you. I don't think the mind gets addicted to suffering. It gets addicted to things that take it away from suffering. Like different types of drugs, alcohol, food, television, gaming, gambling – a whole pile of different things it gets addicted to that take it away from suffering, away from pain. I don't think it gets addicted to suffering, no.

~

S: If someone betrays me, I always feel I have to have revenge in some way. How can I let this pattern go because I see it just causes me suffering?

V: Okay, if someone betrays me yeah, yeah, why would you want to do that? Human beings do betray. I don't actually have a belief system that they shouldn't because it's human nature to betray. It's "what is" in the world. Humans betray. I don't have a belief system that they shouldn't. And as a result of not having a belief system that they shouldn't betray me, I don't contract or go into resistance when they do. And they do. But I don't contract over it. I don't go into resistance. I don't think revengeful thoughts or get bitter or resentful. It's just what is. It's human nature.

Somehow, when people betray you, it touches you and you feel pain so you want to get people back for the pain. Well, that's pretty unconscious. Become more conscious and have a look. Have a look inside of yourself. What's actually happening inside of you? Someone betrays you. Something gets touched. It hurts so you want to hurt someone back. Not very loving. Not very caring. Not very mature.

How many people have you betrayed? People say, "Well, I don't betray." If you're in a relationship with someone and you've had a pornographic thought about someone else, that's betrayal. When people tell me they haven't betrayed, it's like "Really? Really?" It's human nature to betray. What is it? "He who hath not sinned, let him or her cast the first stone," as Jesus said.

~

S: Is even the desire to be enlightened suffering?

V: Heck yeah. That desire creates a great deal of suffering, but it is the one and only desire that is worth having. Because the desire to be enlightened is the desire that will get you free. All other desires pretty much create suffering for you and don't present a great deal of results. But the desire for freedom, the desire for Enlightenment, the thirst for Truth is the only desire that should be totally 100 per cent supported because that one can get you out of jail. That one can get you out of the matrix of your mind. You'll know yourself as Truth. That desire is worth everything. That thirst is worth promoting.

S: The next question is from Satya.

V: Hi Satya.

S: Hello Vishrant. Vishrant, my question is: physical illness, does it affect our consciousness?

V: Can do. It depends what the physical illness is, how it affects the mind. I had hepatitis when I was about 33 or 34, I think, and it affected me a great deal because it made me very, very ill and I had to stay in bed for six months. And it affected my consciousness brilliantly because I just meditated for six months. So yes, physical illness can really affect your consciousness.

S: And Vishrant, due to physical illness people like someone having high blood pressure or diabetes, when they take these kinds of medicines, does it also affect the body and the level of consciousness?
V: Can do, depending on what the drug is. A great deal depends on how the drug that they're taking affects the mind, but the mind can learn surrender. And once it's learned surrender, it's learned all it needs to learn for higher consciousness and for Enlightenment.
S: Okay, thank you, Vishrant.
V: Okay, thank you Satya.
~
S: Can you explain what betrayal means?
V: Betrayal? So, you're in relationship with someone, and you have a deal whereby you guys don't sleep around, you just sleep with each other, and your partner decides to go and sleep with someone else without telling you. That would mean that you've been betrayed because the deal you had with each other has been broken. The commitment you had with each other – to be just with each other – has been broken. There's been a betrayal.
S: Why is having a pornographic thought about someone other than our partner betrayal?
V: Because it is.
S: I consider myself reasonably happy. Do you think I'm fooling myself and don't even see my own suffering?
V: Most people don't see their own suffering. I don't know what you're like. You might be a very happy

person. But most people don't recognise that every desire they have is a form of suffering because it's resistance. Most people don't recognise it. Every time they get frightened of losing something, they're suffering because it happens so much. They don't realise that it's suffering. If you are in a desireless state, you don't suffer. So have a look and see. Have a look and see. Every thought you have that involves you wanting something to be different than how it is is a form of resistance, is a form of suffering, even if it's mild.

Now, if we addictively demand something, we suffer incredibly. If we go into massive resistance to anything, we suffer incredibly. But you've got to have a look. You've got to get ruthlessly honest with yourself and see, how is your mind working? What is it actually doing?

A lot of people keep themselves away from the feelings inside of themselves that are unpleasant through hope: the hope that somehow things are going to be better later. Now, that's just a dream. It's kind of like a drug that people take to keep them away from reality – the reality of what's here now. If we take away all of our future projections and just live in the now, what's actually here? What's our mind doing? What's it been programmed to do? And I gotta tell you, none of us at school were programmed to be happy. We were programmed to be efficient little machines, solving problems. That worked very well for us at school because we got to pass exams and get certificates or whatever we needed to go on, but unfortunately, that usually continues until we die.

And every time we go into resistance to anything, it is a form of suffering. It is a form of dissatisfaction. But because we've become so used to it, we don't notice it until the mind stops, and then you see it. Meditation facilitates the stopping of the mind, the quietening of the mind. And then you see it.

S: So there is no way to be without suffering without an equanimous mind?

V: You want to stop suffering? Wake up. Or stop resisting life. That'll do. It's up to you. You're creating it. You're creating the suffering. You can stop it. Stop resisting life. Be free. Accept life as it is. Stop taking offence. Stop being a victim. These are all things you create. And they're all things that are within your control. You create your reality by the way you think. So if you're creating suffering through resistance, stop it.

S: The next question: how can I drown out my negative thinking?

V: Okay, so yeah, if you're a negative thinker, you've been programmed to be a negative thinker. When I first got into personal growth, it was all about being a positive thinker and developing positive thinking patterns. It didn't take me long to realise that that's actually not a requirement because people, human beings, are naturally buoyant. We're born naturally buoyant. The only thing that sinks us is negative thinking. We don't need positive thinking. But negative thinking definitely sinks us.

I first started changing negative patterns in my life when I was 19. One of them was victim-orientated thinking, which is negative thinking, being a victim of this, being a victim of that, being a victim of myself, being a victim of someone else, being a victim of a situation. That's negative thinking, so I stopped that. It took years because I was a great victim, but I just refused to be a victim and I stopped it. Anytime a victim-orientated thought would arise in my mind, I'd just stop it.

The other negative program that I saw that was hurting me was worry. Worry is negative programming as well, because it just hurts you and does not change a thing. As Saint Francis of Assisi stated: "It does not make you an inch taller." No amount of worry can. That was the second thing that I stopped. Anytime worry arose in my mind, I just stopped it. But it's up to you.

You're asking to drown out negative thinking? That sounds negative in itself. Just stop it. You find yourself being negative? Stop it. Every time it arises, stop it until it doesn't come anymore. Whatever we feed in our mind grows. If you feed the negative thinking, it grows. Stop it. Atrophy it. Up to you. And it's not going to be easy. If you're a negative thinker, it's going to be difficult to change those default patterns. But what else have you got to do? It's the best thing you can do. Raise your consciousness levels. Stop thinking negatively, because negative thinking does not raise consciousness levels. It keeps you locked in lower consciousness and suffering. You're in control of your mind. Nobody else. It's up to you.

S: Can positive thinking help us with openness whilst we are learning openness?

V: I don't promote positive thinking. I don't promote any form of thinking, really. Positive thinking? Nah. Just don't negatively think. Human beings are naturally buoyant. Just don't negatively think. Any negative thoughts arise, discount them, and you'll find that you'll be buoyant. You don't need positive thinking. Just don't get involved in negative thinking.

S: What do you mean when you say human beings are naturally buoyant?

V: I don't know if you've ever been involved with small children – having your own or being involved with maybe someone else's – but they're naturally buoyant. Oh, we're born buoyant. We're born bouncy. We're born "up". We're not born down. We're resilient. I think it's part of the survival mechanism, being a human being. It's not until we develop negative ways of thinking that we sink ourselves. Have a look for yourself. Find a relative or someone when he's got a little kid. See how buoyant they are. You would have been like that when you were little as well, so what happened?

S: The next question is from a viewer: Do you believe that human beings should only be attracted and attached to one person and that any other energy is betrayal?

V: Ah, somewhere you're thinking that I think betrayal is bad. I just think it's what human beings do. I don't categorise it as good or bad. It's just what human beings do. They do betray. It's human nature to betray. If you have a look at your own mind, you'll see that it betrays. If you're not honest with yourself, you won't see it, but it betrays. To actually think that other human beings shouldn't betray you is actually out of touch with reality. It's delusional.

As far as being attracted to one person... of course, you can be attracted to as many people as you like. I was just suggesting that we all betray and I was using an example that if we are in a relationship where we are committed, and we actually have pornographic thoughts about someone else, that's a form of betrayal. It was just an indicator that shows that we do betray. It's human nature to betray. I'm not making a statement that we shouldn't be attracted or you're not attracted to more than one person, because that would also be out of touch with nature, because we probably are. I'm just stating that human beings betray. It's part of their nature.

~

S: When we are perceiving love more of the time, is that an indicator we are resisting life less?
V: Yes.

~

S: How do I stop the habitual pattern of seeing myself as a victim of circumstances?
V: How the world has wronged me? Yeah, that's victim-orientated thinking. That's one of the first things, when I was 19, I decided to change because quite often people who are victim-orientated are angry people because they take offence and they blame. They get angry. I was an angry young man, and I could see how destructive that was. And I could see clearly that it was created by my victim-orientated

thinking and it's easy to see people as wronging you because we can get very critical. But anytime we take offence, we're creating suffering for ourselves. I just really saw the point that to be a victim of anything is a voluntary act. Bad things may happen, but you have to put your hand up to be a victim of them. It's a choice. People think it's not a choice. Yes, it is a choice. We create ourselves as victims or we create ourselves as not. I just see life as it is. Not good, not bad, just as it is. You want to see yourself as a victim? Well, you'll suffer until you die. Because there's always going to be things to blame for how you feel. You're the one doing it to you though. Nobody else is doing it to you. You're responsible for your feelings: 100 per cent responsible.

S: Is being a victim based on our belief systems or is it just programming?

V: Yes, based on your belief systems. I'll give you an example of that. Look, I remember when I was quite young, I was mugged in Perth city by a couple of bikies, and at that time I was quite young. I think I was 18 or something. Maybe even 17, I don't know. It was pretty young. And these bikies, they beat me up and they, they mugged me, they stole my money. And I got to have a really good look at that, you know. It's like, now, these guys have beaten me up. And they've stolen my money and I'm sore. Now, I can be a victim of that and hurt myself with those thoughts or I can see this is just what it is. And I saw the choice. I saw a choice there. Now, if I become a victim of it, I'm gonna hurt myself more and more and more because I'm likely to run that story of being beaten up and robbed over and over again, and every time I do, I'm going to stab myself. Or I cannot be a victim of it, by choice, and see it just is what is, not rotate the story over and over again and hurt myself over and over again. Because they did what they did once. Now, I can do it to myself over and over again, by being a victim, by thinking I'm a victim, and I just chose not to. I just chose not to be a victim. Because I couldn't see the point. I'd already been robbed. I'd already been beaten up. Why did I have to do it to myself over and over and over again, by running victim-orientated thoughts about it? I didn't. It was a choice, so I chose not to be a victim.

S: Did your mind still bring the stories up and then you just dismissed them?

V: No, because I had chosen not to be a victim. I moved to acceptance of what had occurred and the stories disappeared. If we are holding someone in contempt for what they've done – in other words, being a victim of them – we're likely to run the story over and over again. But if we move to acceptance, the situation is pretty much over. Acceptance destroys story. As long as we remain the victim though, there's a story. When life is just what is, story's over. Have a look.

It's up to you. I'm not talking about what's fair and what's not fair here. I'm just talking about you not creating suffering for you. That's all I'm talking about. Because when we turn ourselves into a victim, we're the ones hurting ourselves. What's happened has already happened. But now we're hurting ourselves because of the way we think about it. Have a look.

S: When that happened, had you been practising acceptance for some time?

V: Not necessarily acceptance, but I had spent a lot of time alone as a teenager. And a lot of time in contemplation. I used to walk at night time. I used to walk for hours at night time, just looking at life, wondering about this and wondering about that. And I got to walk with violence. I got to walk with trying to understand violence against me. And I just got to see clearly there was a correlation between me actually being physically hurt and me creating my own suffering. And then I got this book called The Handbook to Higher Consciousness by Ken Keyes and he talked about this victim orientation and how it works in the mind. And it just all clicked. It's like, yeah, we create our own reality by the way we think. Bad things can happen to us. We can be a victim of those bad things or not. Our choice. If we choose to be a victim of those things that have happened to us, we will hurt ourselves over and over and over again. The person who did it to us or whatever, they're not doing it anymore. We're doing it to us now. We're doing it to ourselves. And I just saw it and I chose not to do it. I chose not to hurt myself by being a victim.

S: It is time.

V: Ah, it is time. Thank you for satsang. Good to see you bravehearts here today.

CHAPTER SIX

The Only Chance Humanity Has to Survive

V: Welcome to satsang.
S: Hello Vishrant. Can you please talk about the only chance humanity has to survive?
V: Well, we've got to look at the reasons why there's trouble, why humanity is destroying the atmosphere, why wars are being threatened, why terrorist acts are happening. We've got to look at the reasons, basic reasons, why these are happening – and from my perspective, it is simply lower consciousness. People are operating out of lower consciousness rather than higher consciousness. People operating out of higher consciousness would be taking care of the planet. They would be more interested in building bridges than building tanks, submarines and other weapons. As long as lower consciousness reigns in the halls of power, there's a problem because lower consciousness dictates an "us" and a "them" and really there is only an "us". We're on this little planet, all of us, but there's greed, there's power trips, there's lies, there's deception, there's all sorts of things going on that belong to the category of lower consciousness.

My interest is in helping people raise their consciousness levels because this is the only chance. Unfortunately, you can't do it en masse, you can only do it with those who are interested in raising their consciousness levels. So that's what's attempted here. If you raise your consciousness levels, you can't be involved in violence. You can't be involved in greed. You can't be involved in power tripping because your consciousness levels dictate this is ridiculous. As a matter of fact, more than likely, if your consciousness levels are high, you're involved in loving everybody: the good, the bad, and the ugly. This is what happens when you raise your consciousness levels. You find love. And you find love for everybody, not just the people who are close to you, not just your family, but everybody. Humanity has this opportunity to raise its consciousness levels at this time because there's so much going on that is detrimental for the future of our children, but whether they'll do that or not, I don't know. It's up to you as an individual. Getting angry and protesting about the way things are doesn't help. That's just lower consciousness as well.

People then want to know, well, how do we raise our consciousness levels? It begins by watching your own mind, by witnessing your own mind, because if you can see what you're up to, if you can see all of your agendas, all your defence systems, all your programming, you can then see others, you can see the world and you know that we're all the same. We're all the same. We've all got the same stuff. We look at people and we judge them, but the truth is the judgments are probably wrong. There for the grace of God goes I, depending on what patterning or programming that person has. It's up to you as an individual, if you want to help the planet, to raise your consciousness levels. Not to get out there and get angry. That doesn't work. That's just adding more darkness to the darkness that's already here. Raise your consciousness levels. This is best. There's nothing better actually. That's it.

Any questions, any statements, any challenges to this teaching today?

S: The first question: Do you think the human species has become more conscious in the last few decades?

V: Heck no. Look, I don't think so. I think there's a New Age movement that thinks there's some kind of quickening or awakening around the planet, but I don't think so. It doesn't seem that way to me. There doesn't seem to be more light on this planet. There seems to be more darkness, if anything. We're seeing people on Facebook and other media talking about waking up to what is, becoming wiser to what's going on around the world, but they're coming from a place of anger. They're coming from a place of closure. That's not higher consciousness, that's lower consciousness. Waking up has nothing to do with having some nasty dream and getting angry about it. Higher consciousness is very beautiful. You find a way to accept everyone and everything, and in that there is peace.

S: If it's true that higher consciousness would help us win in the material world, would you say that politicians have higher consciousness to be able to get to the top?

V: I don't know any politicians so I can't make a judgement call on that. That's not possible for me.

I tend to keep away from politics. I don't have an interest in them. I have an interest in helping people wake up. That's about it.

S: The next question has been written by Steven: Hello Vishrant. Given what you've said about needing to raise consciousness levels, how do we encourage people to want to do this?

V: Well Steven, that's what I'm doing right now. I'm talking about the subject. The positive side of raising consciousness levels is that we have a beautiful planet and we have beautiful people sharing this planet with us. The downside of not raising the consciousness levels doesn't look good. It looks like the environment is going to get destroyed for humanity. It looks like there could be wars. It looks like there could be famines. It looks like there could be terrorism. This is all lower consciousness. This is not higher consciousness. The best you can do for the planet is raise your consciousness level because if you raise your consciousness levels, you become a light so others can see. That's the best you can do.

S: The next question is from Susha.

S: Hi Vishrant.

V: Hello Susha.

S: Vishrant, what keeps me in lower consciousness is my need for being somebody. How can I deal with that?

V: So being a somebody is an ego-based reality for all people who are ego-based. They think they're a somebody. That "somebody" is made up of projection based on previous experience and belief systems. It's not real. It seems very real, but it's not real. Take away your imagination and you as a somebody don't exist. You as an "I" don't exist. What you can learn to do is put yourself aside for the benefit of others, move into service of others. In moving into service and putting yourself aside, there is less and less and less of you, and as a result of this less and less and less of you, your life is more beautiful. Selfless service is a beautiful way to live in this world. It is not beautiful to live in this world selfishly. It is beautiful to live in this world, in the Way of the Heart, as a giver, as a caretaker. This is lovely. Usually, this involves raising your consciousness levels because selfishness belongs to lower consciousness and selflessness belongs to higher consciousness.

S: Yeah, you've said this so many times, but it finally struck a chord. That's the perfect way for me to put myself aside.

V: Yeah, and it doesn't have to be for people, though. You can put yourself aside for anything. It could be flowers, it could be animals, it could be anything. It's just the story of you is always a story of problems and when we go into problem solving, we're going into lower consciousness again. We're going into dream.

S: Problem solving is part of my job which is hard to put aside.

V: No, it's part of my job also, but I don't live there. When I need to problem solve, I problem solve. When I don't, my mind is silent. Unless you want to make problem solving every waking minute and then it's a real problem because that's what we learned to do at school, isn't it? We learned to problem solve so we'd get good marks and get a certificate of some kind and we could get a good job. Do we really need to continue that until we die?

S: Not really. Not at all. Thank you Vishrant. Thank you.

V: Like, just as you're sitting here, just as you're sitting here with me, are there any problems?

S: No.

V: I noticed that too. There are no problems. Unless you want to bring a problem into your mind, into your thoughts, and then then you think it's real. Really, there's nothing happening.

S: That's true. Nothing's happening.

V: Nothing's happening.

S: Especially tuning into you, nothing is happening. Thank you so much.

V: Thank you, Susha.

~

S: I've noticed that there are many people today who are getting out of their religions and questioning their own belief systems that were instilled into them. Would you call that a sign of higher consciousness?

V: If they were getting into higher consciousness, yes, but are they getting into higher consciousness by dropping certain belief systems around religions? Are they actually getting into higher consciousness? I don't know. I don't know if that's true.

S: I've got another question. In the previous satsang that I attended you mentioned that there is no free will and we operate based on our programming, but

I've heard you say things like "it's up to you" or "it's your choice," but how can I have a choice if there's no free will?

V: Okay. So I have to talk in a way where people understand me, and people believe they have free will and when you talk in a way where it doesn't sound like they have free will, they won't understand me. I've got to use the English language and I've got to use it in a way that is heard by people. I have to talk in a manner so people understand me. My world is a world of silence and stillness. I come to your world, which is the world of words and dream, to talk to you about freedom. Your world is a world of prison. The mind is a prison, the bars of which are made of fear, and I've come to talk to you about that. I have to use your language and the way that you put words together for you to understand me, even though sometimes that might not be 100 per cent correct. I'm still stuck with the English language which is an ego-based language. So it's difficult.

We don't have any free will. That's not possible. You're running true to your patterning. You're running true to your programs. You are getting influenced by what's being said and that influence may change your patterning, but once again, the influence is coming from outside of you, not from inside of you. I'm playing with parts of you that may change things inside of you, but they were already there. They're already programmed into you. I'm just trying to tap into them so you'll go for freedom, so you'll go and do something to raise your consciousness levels. And once again, the programming is coming externally, in this case from me. So it makes sense.

S: Yes, it does. Alright, and one more question. Last time, someone asked if humans are the only beings that are capable of Enlightenment and in response to that, you mentioned that animals have the potential to be awakened when they become humans in their next life. Do you believe in reincarnation?

V: Reincarnation is not a belief on my part. It's a knowing. I remember hundreds of lives on this planet and I remember them like I remember this life, very clearly. I started remembering when I was about 11 years old. At that time, I was a Roman Catholic schoolboy and it just didn't make sense to me. I discounted it really strongly, but it kept coming back over and over again. The same story about my previous life, the same memories. I started to look at it more closely and realised there is something in this, and then the other lives started to appear. People think you remember all of the good stuff. You remember how wonderful you were. No, you remember all of the tragedy. You remember the sorrow. You remember the bloodshed. You remember all of the traumatic events. That's what you remember, and in remembering that, I really did not want to do this here again.

S: Right, and the forms in which we will be reincarnated, will they be forms of other life forms or will they be only human forms?

V: I think that we can regress and we can improve. We can go back and we can improve and so I think it's possible for people to regress back to animal form.

S: Right. And one more question. Are all enlightened individuals capable of leaving their bodies at their own will and why do they do it if it's true?

V: I really don't know the answer to that question. I'm pretty sure if I wanted to die, I could die, but I don't know. We'll have to try it and see. Get back to me after I'm dead.

S: Okay. All right.

V: Yeah, see these questions won't help you much. They're just curiosity questions. Learn to surrender and get free and you learn to accept surrender by accepting life as it is. Learn to do that and get free. Practise acceptance and get free. Collecting knowledge, particularly this sort of superficial knowledge, won't help you much. It actually won't help you at all, really.

S: Right, I will try my best.

V: As Yoda said, "Do or do not, there is no try."

S: All right, okay. Thank you. Thank you.

~

S: The next question has been written by Rita: It feels like there are vested interests trying to keep humanity in lower consciousness to exploit humanity or is it a collective consciousness problem? And there seem to be fewer awake people like yourself.

V: So you've given me an alternative question, the alternative answer question, and the truth is I don't know. People think that when you wake up, you know all of these things. I don't know. I really don't know. The more I see, the more I realise I don't know, and this is one of those questions. I don't know whether humanity is going to become more conscious or not. I don't know whether it's supposed to. I don't know. Whether it has in the past and has gone backwards? I don't know. I just don't know.

The reason people want to know is because they want to control things. And I don't have an interest in controlling things so I'm quite happy with "I don't know".

S: The next question is as follows: Scientists say that we're in great danger of destroying the environment we live in so it won't be suitable for human life. How come we are not able to hear that warning and make significant change?

V: The people in power who have the power to change it don't want to hear it because it's expensive. It's that simple. It's about money. It's about greed. It's about power. They don't want to hear it because it's expensive. Very short-sighted view.

S: Why do modern leaders serve power, not love?

V: To serve love, you have to be open. And you have to be really wide open to perceive love. I doubt very much whether our leaders are wide open. I'd say they're quite defended while pretending to be open. Well, they won't be perceiving much love. True love is perceived in openness, not in closure.

S: Why do people elect leaders that serve power and not love?

V: Because they want to. They don't know the difference themselves. In a lot of cases, people put forward an idea of themselves which they promote through the media, through advertising and whatever else, and people buy it because they're gullible. They buy it because they want to. My understanding of politics is that they're pretty ugly. People not meaning what they say and not saying what they mean a lot.

To find someone who truly loves humanity would be rather rare. To find people who truly love, you have to find people who are truly open. That in itself is a rarity, to find people who are truly open. People can say they love, but if they're closed, they're probably not perceiving it. If they're highly defended, they're probably not perceiving it. That won't be happening. We don't live in a society that promotes love. We live in a society that promotes success, power and money. But you as an individual can change. Only you as an individual can change. You can open up. You can start watching your mind. You can start with your mind. You can practise the Way of the Heart. You can. Thinking that the whole planet should change? Well, no. Yet how about you? Just you, you do it. That's best.

~

S: Vishrant, good morning again.
V: Hello Steven.
S: I just want to say thank you. I think the last couple of sentences that you've given us are my message for today. I think it is up to us. From what I gather from you, it is up to us to become more aware and I think that's enough for me to do. I'd like to just thank you for that. I think it's the best message that I've got from today so far. So I just wanted to thank you. I will leave now and go on working on awareness today.

And obviously, everybody else here will also be able to do the same.
V: Thank you, Steven. You know, I never expect anyone to hear me, Steven. So it's nice that you have.
S: Thank you Vishrant. Stay well.

~

S: The next question is as follows: I find it hard to not get righteous when I see people throwing plastic trash into nature or other harmful behaviours for the planet. How do you not get righteous about behaviours that are obviously wrong?
V: Well, what I do is I pick the trash up and put it in the bin.

What's the point of getting righteous? What's the point? How does that help anyone? How does that help the consciousness levels on the planet? You want to help the planet? Pick the trash up and put it in a bin. That works.
S: When trying to make the world a better place, how do you not get hopeless in front of so much impenetrable ignorance from people?
V: Hopelessness is a future projection. I don't have a great deal of interest in the future, really, particularly thinking about it. There's now – and now is really nice. Why entertain negativity? Why entertain anything of the future really? There's just now. This is good enough. And the truth is, we can only ever live in the now.

Anything that comes with regards to the future is a projection. It's not real. It's a dream. It's a nasty dream you're having or it might be a nice dream, but it's a dream. There is only now. It's nice to live in the now. It is not nice to live in projections, whether they're hopeful or hopelessness, because it's all rubbish. There's only now.

S: A viewer from YouTube writes: My question is, what is the ultimate question? If this hasn't been asked.

V: The ultimate question is always the same question: "Who am I?" asked to yourself. "Who am I, really?" Because if you discover who you are – in other words, if awareness becomes aware of itself, Beingness becomes aware of itself – you become a light so others may see. This is the ultimate question. Who am I? It is also the last question.

S: What do you mean by the last question?

V: Well, once you discover who you are, that's it. You're free. There's nothing more to know. It's over, people don't get that. They think, "Oh, I'll wake up and then I'll do this or I'll do that". No, you have no idea. If you wake up, what's happened is you've given your life to Truth and then Truth will do what it wants with your life. You as an "I" drop. You're gone. People get this silly idea that they're going to wake up and then they're going to do something afterwards, as though there's somehow some continuation of the ego. No, it drops. The true you lives. Beingness lives. The false you drops. The dream drops. It's not like the dream wakes up. The "I" doesn't wake up. That's not possible. It doesn't wake up because it was never real in the first place. That that's aware of the dream becomes aware of itself. That's Enlightenment if it's ongoing.

S: The next question is: Since human beings have been hunting and eating meat for thousands of years, do you think we have the right to kill animals?

V: Depends where your consciousness levels are at, really. At some point, if your consciousness level goes up high enough, you love all things. You love everything. You don't have conditional love, you have unconditional love because you're open enough to support that. And in unconditional love you can't really – or you won't really, that's a better way of putting it – be involved any kind of cruelty to animals, whether it's killing them or anything else.

At some point, you recognise that no animal put their hand up and said, "Please kill me and eat me". We actually have to murder them basically and steal their most valuable possession, which is their life, so that we can eat them. At some point, your consciousness levels go up high enough for you not to be wanting to be involved in that because you love them, and love dictates that you take care of everything and everyone.

~

S: Hi Vishrant. I notice that when I share with my friends, I only share my good pictures. It further increases the identification to this body. I've been seeing this since some time and accepted that too. I cannot find the underlying belief here. Can you please comment?

V: Well, there doesn't need to be a belief. You're looking for acceptance and that's a primal imperative. It's a part of our survival mechanism to be accepted by our tribe because once upon a time, to not be accepted by our tribe would have meant death. In wanting to show our best side, in wanting to show the pictures that are good, we're looking for acceptance. This doesn't demand belief systems. It's just a primal imperative. It is wonderful when you decide that it doesn't matter if people accept you or not, because then you can be free of all of this. Have a look at it. Have a look at yourself and your need for acceptance. What would you be like if you didn't have that need? If you made it okay for people to not accept you as well as accept you? And ultimately, what other people think of you is none of your business anyway.

I got into this when I was pretty young, you know. If people accept me, that's great. People don't accept me? That's equally great. I seriously don't care.

~

S: Do you think consciousness always finds a way to manifest in the universe?
V: I have no idea. I really don't know. Do I think? I'm not really big on thinking. I'm not really big on philosophising. I like silence and I like stillness. It's really, really, really beautiful.

~

S: Hi Vishrant. Vishrant, you said that we need not look for the acceptance of others. So in that process, we have to make ourselves okay to be lonely?
V: Okay, yep, that'll work. Okay to be not acceptable. How's that? When we're okay with not being acceptable, we can really play. People who are constantly going for the acceptance of others are constantly

twisting themselves into knots to get that approval. They're not really free to just play. You give up trying to get other people's acceptance and you can play because it doesn't matter what people think of you then. You can be the fool. You can have fun.

S: Yes, to be seen as a fool is another fear.

V: Yeah, if people don't like you, that's their problem, not yours. And if people do like you, that's also their problem, not yours.

S: Yeah, yeah. Thank you very much Vishrant. Thank you.

V: Your name Abhayi means fearless. To be okay with people not accepting you takes courage, Abhayi.

S: It's a very beautiful name you have given me. It always reminds me.

V: That's exactly what it's for, to remind you to step through your fears and have a good life, a full life. Celebrate life.

S: Thank you very much Vishrant.

V: Thank you.

~

S: Is it a problem to have fun at the expense of others sometimes?

V: Oh, what a question! Is it a problem to have fun at the expense of others? Life is such a joke. You know, just have a look in the mirror and you'll see one looking back at you. The things we do, the things we get up to – if you can't laugh at yourself and you can't have a laugh with other people, life is just too hard. It's such a joke this whole world. Laugh as much as you can, as often as you can. It's best.

S: Did you ever have to practise not taking offence?
V: Yeah, I did, when I was learning about not hurting myself. I had to learn not to take offence. The moment we take offence to anything, anyone, we are now hurting ourselves and we are responsible for that hurt, not the other. The other is just doing what the other does. The other is the world. The world does what the world does. When we take offence, we are now hurting ourselves because we are 100 per cent responsible for our reaction.

~

S: Hello Vishrant, thanks for answering my question. After I had posted the question, I was thinking that this is not related to the topic. And I had this fear of appearing like a fool, as Abhayi was mentioning, and I was just going to say to Tosh, don't include that question. In the meantime, you answered the question. So yeah, I don't know why I have this fear of appearing foolish in front of other people.
V: Because you won't be accepted if you appear as a fool. People won't accept you. It comes back to that survival mechanism of acceptance. The thing is, if you are willing to be seen as a fool, you can have an awful lot of fun. There's no fun in trying to be constantly serious and constantly accepted by others. There's no fun in that. But boy, is there fun when you're willing to be seen as the fool. You can really enjoy this life. You can celebrate it fully. I decided, gosh, 30 years ago to become God's fool.
S: That's really good. And whenever I'm scared of something, I'm trying to come forward. I'm trying

to see what my fears are. I'm scared of too much. I am scared of public speaking and other things, but I'm pushing myself and trying to overcome the fear and see it.

V: Yeah, step through it. Instead of obeying the fear, use courage and step through it. When we obey fear, we kind of lose. We learn about everything. By the time we're 20 we know what's dangerous. We know what's not dangerous. We don't really need fear to protect us anymore, but it continues on until the body dies, unless you wake up. So you can obey it or not obey it, but if you obey it, you're not gonna have much of a life because fear will have you do nothing. You'll have you be safe all of the time.

S: Yes. Thank you, Vish. Thanks a lot.

V: Nice to talk to you.

S: Yeah, I love you so much Vishrant. Thank you.

V: Love to you, my dear.

~

S: Speaking of taking responsibility for your feelings, what is the experience of being hurt like when you take full responsibility for your own feelings?

V: If you're taking responsibility for your feelings, there's been a touch. Something's touched you and there's been a pain. Now, when we don't take responsibility, we tend to blame and now we're in a victim-orientated mode and we've gone to blame and now we're hurting ourselves. You have a look. Something happens. There's a touch. Quite often in human beings there's an instant reaction of blame. Turning ourselves into a victim of somebody or something is not required. Just allow yourself to have the touch. Stop reacting. Allow yourself to own the touch. Be responsible. Be mature. Anytime that we're blaming others for how we feel, we're being immature because we make ourselves feel. Nobody could make me feel but me. People may do things I don't like, I don't agree with – maybe even damaging – but only I can make me feel and I'm responsible for that.

S: Does the blame always occur in the form of mental talk or chatter or can it be something pre-verbal or energetic?

V: Yeah, it can be an instantaneous reaction. Like anger, for instance's sake, can be instantaneous, but if we truly dissect anger, we find that anger is a reaction that stops us from feeling something. Someone does something. It touches. Anger arises. In the anger, we don't have to feel the touch so much because we've been empowered by the anger which is supported by blame. Without blame, anger can't continue.

Blame is the fuel that anger needs to survive. The moment we remove blame and take responsibility for ourselves, anger dies. So yeah, there can be an instant reaction. At some point that closes down too, as consciousness levels rise. Instead of reacting, you're actually just detached and you're with the touch, you're not reacting anymore. You're not going to blame anymore. But that takes higher consciousness. That takes practice.

S: In the removal of the pattern of blaming, does that mean that we'll be feeling the touches more and more?

V: Probably. Particularly if you're wounded. If you're carrying wounding from your past, the touches are going to be hard. That's one of the reasons it's such a great idea to heal the wounds of your Heart by allowing yourself to feel them when they do get triggered instead of finding a way to avoid that feeling. If all we do is avoid the feelings when we get touched by life, we have to spend our whole life avoiding. How about being tenderly okay with whatever appears, always, without going to blame, without reaction, to be tenderly okay with everything that appears? This will heal you. This is the way.

~

S: The next question is as follows: Is it enough to have leaders that serve love or would our entire population need to start to serve love to save humanity?
V: Why don't you serve love and see where it takes you? Worrying about what other people are going to do or not going to do isn't going to solve any problems. Why don't you serve love and see where that takes you? Make a difference yourself. Stop relying on other people to make a difference and you make a difference. That's best.

S: How come so few people have Heart on this planet?
V: I think everyone's capable of love. It's just that most people are pretty closed. If you're closed, it's very hard to perceive love. A lot of people make the mistake of thinking that caring and gentleness and kindness are love when they're really aspects of the mind. When the mind is affected by love, those aspects do tend to come out, but not necessarily. With

love, because people can learn and have patterns of kindness, caring, gentleness, they then think that's love, but not necessarily. True love occurs in openness. When you're wide open, you can perceive love. In the meantime, your mind can pretend to be love and pretend to love. Mind is really capable of an awful lot of pretence. It can pretend to be silent, pretend to be love. The imagination of the mind is brilliant. The only difference between that and the real deal is true silence never gets stale. True love never gets stale. It's always fresh. It's always beautiful. It's always lovely.

~

S: Is going for Enlightenment a way to save humanity?

V: Heck yeah. Yes, sacrifice yourself for humanity. That's the shot. Because in Enlightenment the mind needs to surrender unconditionally. You surrender your life so others may see. That's brilliant. That's a good idea. Yeah, why not? There's no such thing as selfish Enlightenment. You don't wake up as an "I" and stay awake. That's not possible. Awakening occurs and the "I" drops. You want to sacrifice your life, you want to learn unconditional surrender and practise it? Practise it so others may see. That's a brilliant way to go. That's the Way of the Heart.

~

S: Do you ever get a sense of helplessness because you can only do so much within your sphere of influence?

V: I don't deal in helplessness or hopelessness. They're mind trips, I'm just not interested. What is is what is, and it's here now. I have no interest in future projections. What is is what is, and for myself, it's all okay. Everything is okay as it is. As a matter of fact, it's more than that, it's perfect – perfection upon perfection upon perfection. Now, if you want to understand that statement, find yourself as Truth, and you'll see it clearly.

~

S: We were talking before about feeling the touches. Is there ever a point where nothing touches or there's no more touch?

V: I haven't felt a great deal of touch for a long time. I don't know the answer to that. There's no rejection of touches, just detachment really from everything. It's part of the deal. Awareness becomes aware of itself. The mind is very detached from everything. It's just how it is. Most of the time I spend in silent bliss. I recommend Enlightenment to all my friends. It's brilliant. There's nothing better to go for on this plane as a human being. Go for freedom. Go for Enlightenment. Go for higher consciousness. Everything else is just repetitive. You've done it so many times before. Go for freedom, raise your consciousness levels. That's best. There's nothing better.

Everybody here that you know who's ego-based is imprisoned and they're suffering and they will suffer till they die and then they will do it again. Get free. Go for Enlightenment. Go for higher consciousness. Give it your totality. This is the best you can do for you and the best you can do for everybody you know.

Thank you for satsang. Good to see you bravehearts here today.

CHAPTER SEVEN

The Peace in Becoming No One

V: Welcome to satsang.
S: Hello Vishrant, can you please talk about the peace in becoming no one?
V: You already are no one. It's not like you're a somebody, really. Without your imagination, you don't exist. So becoming no one is not a possibility because you already are a no one.

My experience with being a no one is that it happens after awakening. It doesn't happen before awakening. Before awakening, you're ego-based. There's an "I" there that thinks it's doing something that thinks it's done something and thinks it's going to do something. After awakening, that drops and there's a sense that there's nobody here. There's no one here. There's talking, but there's nobody talking. It's different. And yes, it's peaceful because the noise maker is not here. The "I" – the one who thinks it has a future, thinks it had a past, the one who worries, the one who grieves – is gone. And yeah, peace, profound contentment for no reason. But this is a side effect of Enlightenment, it's not something the ego can actually do because it's an absence of the ego. Awareness is aware of itself and the mind can't possibly believe the ego to be real.

Are there any questions, any statements, any challenges to this teaching today?

S: The first question is from Deepesh.

V: Hello.

S: Yes sir. My question is, for the last many years, I misunderstood the term spirituality. It was a magical moment, when I heard you. You said the term is not right. The Truth is the right thing. And I understood it in a different way. Just like this or last many years, because of the knowledge I can come through also, books and everything, the term surrender was also completely misunderstood. Actually, in your last session, last satsang, you were telling that if you are trying to control your mind, that is not surrender. So could you please suggest to me, in a different way, what is surrender then? How can we achieve this?

V: Okay, well to begin with, surrender is a non-doing, so if someone throws something at you, there's no reaction, there's no doing. There may be a response, but there's no reaction. The mind is surrendered. When someone insults you and there's no movement in the mind, it just stays still – this is surrender. This is a mind that has basically been undone. To get to this, the practice of acceptance of life as it is, acceptance of people as they are, and dropping everything that we hold on to works. But only the practice: no amount of collected knowledge can teach us surrender, no amount of collected knowledge can heal a wound of the Heart. If we practise acceptance of life as it is – all of the things that we don't like – if we practise accepting them, we can learn surrender. And we fail a lot when we're practising. Someone who has been successful at it has just practised a great deal. That's all. Because it's against our survival mechanism to surrender, to be surrendered. It's against our survival mechanism to accept life as it is. We're fighters. We're born as fighters. We're born to resist. But because we're intelligent, we can learn to accept life and learn to drop things, let things go. We can learn to do that. And if we practise it long enough, we get good at. It is as simple as that.

S: Okay, I was communicating with you before, also in the past, and you were suggesting I focus on the breath, and I was trying to study that. Like, it was going well. And every time I was doing something, I was focused on my breath, I was doing my things. I was aware in the marketplace. Yesterday, suddenly, something about the past came in and I couldn't do anything. And it was to that level that I couldn't sleep all night, and like, now, this has continued. So, what can I do with this kind of thing?

V: So you always begin with acceptance. If you can't sleep, you accept that you can't sleep. If your mind is bothering you, you accept that your mind is bothering you. You always begin with acceptance rather than resistance to what is, and in doing so, you're teaching the mind to let go. You're teaching it to stop talking to itself because when we fully accept situations, the mind has nothing to say about it. It's only when we're in resistance to life that the mind is very active, so in learning to accept, in learning to let go, the mind learns to relax. Is there anything more?

S: Oh, I will keep practising. Thank you so much.
V: Nice to talk to you. Nice to talk to you.

~

S: So Vishrant, when you say undo the mind and undo your belief systems, it seems to me that if I had agreed that I was not always right, the whole righteousness, and drop that, it could drop practically every belief system. What do you think about that?
V: I'll bring you back to what I was just saying. It's about acceptance. If we accept life as it is, we can still make moves to change things if we want to, but from a place of openness, rather than a place of closure, and so it's all about acceptance. Not much else really. Can you accept life as it is or are you going to resist it? So if you're having a disagreement with your daughter, for example, can you accept the way she is, accept what she has to say, accept yourself and still not agree? Because you can, and you'll find that if you do it that way, you're practising openness because you'll be coming from openness rather than closure. If all we do is practise closure – I'm right, you're wrong, without acceptance – well basically, it's war. And that doesn't teach the mind anything except war. If we want to learn anything of value – and what I see as valuable is surrender – we have to practise acceptance. It doesn't necessarily mean that we agree with anything. So we can still hold an opinion that something is not correct, but can we do it from a place of acceptance that that's what is, and in a place of openness? And that's what we have to learn.

S: Okay, yes. I feel like my mind is tricky. It jumps to saying I'm wrong, but maybe inside, the behaviour hasn't changed. The openness is not there. Just using the words.

V: Yeah well, you might not be wrong, you might be right.

S: Well, if it comes to my daughter, maybe you're right.

V: But can you bring acceptance into it? Acceptance of her, acceptance of what she's saying, acceptance of what she's doing, and acceptance of yourself at the same time? Acceptance is the key. It teaches the mind to let go. It teaches the mind to relax.

S: Yes, I can try that.

V: Yeah.

S: I can totally try that. And Vishrant, for the last few days, it takes me a very long time to come to the space and it takes me just a few minutes to sit with you to find the space. This is amazing. Thank you so much. Thank you.

V: You're very welcome, Susha. When I was a seeker, I was always wanting to sit with my awakened teachers because what I would have to do would take me two hours in meditation to find the space, but within a few seconds of sitting with one of my awake teachers, I could find it. I used to value that. It allowed me to find home very quickly and allowed a great deal of clarity. The clarity helps in removing the obstacles because you get to see them. You get to see what's in the way. And so satsang allows the clarity for you to see the obstacles that are in the way of the Heart and in the way of Enlightenment. So sitting with someone who's awake is a really good idea.

~

S: The next question is: If I sell my car, house and most of my possessions, have I become a nobody?

V: Heck no. You probably think you're the somebody who sold your car and your possessions and your house. No, that's not how you become a nobody. That's how you become poor, and I was with this amazing awakened man, Osho Rajneesh, who said we need to become like Zorba the Buddha. We need to find the Buddha within, but also the Zorba: be in the marketplace, be out here, have the cars, have the houses, have the possessions, but don't be attached to them. Its the attachment that's the problem, not having things. Having things is fine. It's the attachment that causes the suffering, that causes the imprisonment. There's nothing wrong with having things.

So in Buddhism, quite often the monks will give up everything. They'll just have a saffron robe and a Buddhist begging bowl and maybe some beads, some sandals, bit of bedding, and that's one way to go about it, but I don't teach monks, I teach lay people. I teach people who are in the marketplace, who have jobs, who have families, who have commitments, and there's a way – but being attached to things is a problem. Learning to let go only occurs through practice, nothing else.

S: The next question is from Sarah.

V: Hi, Sarah.

S: Hi, Vish. How are you?

V: I'm always the same, Sarah.

S: My question is: in the last couple of days, I really noticed the mother wound within myself.

V: I'm not sure what that wound would be. I understand you have a definition of the mother wound, but I don't. So could you let me know what that means?

S: Recognising my contractions and belief systems that I recognise that I have mimicked from my mother.

V: You're talking about programming then that you've actually copied off your mother.

S: Okay, yeah.

V: So wounding is a little different. Wounding is where there's actually stored pain somewhere – from trauma or just from repression. On top of that stored pain, there can be belief systems, programs, but the programs themselves aren't wounding.

S: Sure. Okay. Yeah, apologies, wrong wording there. In regards to that recognition from seeing myself, seeing that I have picked up those behaviours from her, is that what is required, to accept those behaviours?

V: Yeah. Oh heck, yeah. This is what set me on the path in a lot of ways. At the age of 19, I got involved in an encounter group and I had a look at my programming. I recognised that a lot of it I'd got from my mother. I realised that a lot of it created suffering in my life, so I went about changing it because I didn't want to continue negative programming that was hurting me.

S: Yeah.

V: My mother was very victim orientated. My whole family was quite victim orientated, so one of the first programs that I changed inside of myself was this victim orientation. I refuse to be a victim. Full stop. Why would I want to be a victim? You have to volunteer to be a victim because basically, things happen, they can be good, they can be bad. If they're bad, it might touch us, something might touch us, but we make ourselves feel, not what's happened. We are totally 100 per cent responsible for our own feelings. The world can't make me feel, only I can make me feel and I'm responsible for that. I can't blame anyone for that, and in not blaming, I'm not being a victim.

That was the first pattern I removed. I saw it was a family pattern and it was a tragic pattern because it just creates nothing but suffering. It changes nothing in the world. I didn't want to keep it so I started changing it. I've got to tell you though, to change that particular pattern took me a couple of years of practice because it was entrenched.

Victim-orientated thinking is very, very prominent in Australian society. It's not uncommon at all to run into people who just want to tell you their sad story about how their life isn't working and then you tell them your sad story about how your life's not working. And this is how a lot of communication happens. But really, every time we do that, we hurt ourselves.

S: I've noticed that there seems to be identical or similar belief patterns projected at certain men which I see to be similar that my mother had in regards to my father.

V: Well, that could be true too. I picked up most of my patterning from my mother because I didn't have that much to do with my dad because he was out a fair bit, but when I examined it, it was a real good idea to remove some of it. There is a beautiful book by Nancy Friday called My Mother Myself that you could read. It talks all about this subject, how we picked up all of our patterns from mum and how those patterns are now hurting us because they're not healthy patterns, and how we will transfer them to our own children if we don't correct them inside ourselves.

When I worked as a psychotherapist, I wouldn't see a client until they'd actually read that book because I wanted them to get an understanding of how they were programmed and why they were programmed and why they are acting out now.

S: Yeah, thank you. I'll acquire a copy.

V: It's up to you. Yeah, one of the things is you can get involved with a lot of groups around the world, in Australia and everywhere else, that are very victim orientated – groups that support people in victim-orientated thinking which creates more wounding and hurts you.

S: I don't need that.

V: No, you don't. The people you hang out with are quite important because they're going to affect you a great deal.

Is there anything else Sarah?

S: No. Thank you Vishrant.

V: Okay, bye bye. Hello Abhayi.

S: Hi Vishrant. Vishrant, why do I find it difficult to practise let-go and openness with the people I know rather than with strangers? It is easier to practise with the strangers.

V: Yeah, I agree, but the reason for it is very simple: the people who are close to you, you care about them and they're the ones who can really get to you because you care. With a stranger, you don't care so much. It's like, you won't be seeing them again, or you won't be seeing them often. Usually, people who you care about are in your life and you're probably going to see them every day.

I learned more about surrender and more about acceptance from my partners than from anyone else because they were in my life. They were the people who could get me. They were the people who could do things and say things that would touch me. Now I could either relax and move to acceptance or I could go into resistance and create suffering for myself. I chose to accept them as they were, to accept what they're doing, to not go into contraction, to not go into resistance. It took quite a long time and a lot of practice, but after a while I got good at it because I practised. So my best teachers in this world were my partners, the people I shared my life with.

S: Yes, that makes a lot of sense. Because they could get me.

V: Absolutely. Anything else Abhayi?

S: That's all. Thank you very much Vishrant.

V: Thank you Abhayi. Nice to talk to you, Abhayi.

S: Nice to talk to you too.

~

S: The next question has been written by Deepesh: Is there any difference between being present with you where you are now and having you live on the Internet? Is the Buddha field the same in the two?

V: Well, I don't know because I'm here and you're there. If I was there and then I could come back here, I could probably tell you, but I can't do that yet. I've heard that some awakened teachers from the past have been able to be in two places at once, but I just haven't got there. So I can't help you with that. I have had reports back from people saying that they are blown away by the presence through the Internet. I have no idea how that works, but it was also my experience when talking to my teachers through the Internet. It's always better to be in the living presence of someone who's awake, it's always better to be close, but if not, if you can't get close, the Internet does hold a transmission. That transmission can give you clarity and expand your mind. It has the potential to give satori. So use it.

~

S: What's the fastest way to attain peace as an ego?

V: Accept life as it is. It's that simple. The moment you accept life, there's peace. The moment you resist life, there is disruption. There is noise, there is pain. Peace? Well, it's actually our true nature. Beingness is peace. But if we want peace of mind, accept life as it is. Stop fighting. Stop resisting. Let go. This works. Resistance, holding on, fighting also works, but it works to make you unhappy. Let go. Let go. Let go.

S: The next question has been written by Kelly: Is it possible for you to describe the stages of how our thinking is formed during the subtle stages so that we can be alert?

V: Thinking tends to be a remembrance from the past. It's all related to what we've learnt before. In being present to the moment, you've left the past behind, you've left the future – well, it hasn't come. Moving into the moment allows a freshness. In the moment, a thought arises, it comes from the nothingness. It comes from programming that has been put in there over a lifetime. You won't get a thought arising in a newborn baby. They haven't developed the patterning yet. They haven't had the history yet to make it relevant. All thoughts come from the past, memory of the past, so the process is just that whatever affects us in the moment reminds us of something. We bring up memory, and then we bring up thought. It's so quick. If you train your mind to be present to what is real, you start finding that thoughts aren't there so much. So as a young man, I started training my mind to be present to what is real. Everything is real, except for what you think. In being present to what is real, there is a great deal of freshness, of peace, of clarity. When all we do is keep our awareness on what we think, we basically live in a dream that kills our clarity, takes us away from what is real, and puts us in touch with a dream that quite often is problematic.

I got to see this when I was very young and I fell in love with the present moment – initially through extreme sports, racing bikes, rallying cars, underwater diving, martial arts, rugby, anything that was dangerous, basically, until I realised that we actually don't have to be in danger to be present. We can train our minds to be present so we don't live constantly in thought. Most people think that you can't do that. They think that, well, thoughts are there all of the time, but really, if you watch your mind, you see there are quite a lot of blanks. There's a lot of times when there aren't any thoughts, you're just there, you're just present. Now, we go to what's aware of that? What's aware of the thoughts? What's aware of the gap between the thoughts? And now we're starting to turn awareness back to itself. What's aware is more important than knowing where the thoughts came from. Thoughts come, they go, like clouds. What's aware of these thoughts? Because that does not come and go. That is always here – and when awareness turns back on itself, home has been found. Thoughts are just a distraction. They're like looking at the clouds in the sky and missing the sky. Let's see what the sky is like. You've had looking at the clouds for long enough. Whether thoughts come from here or they come from there or how they're processed, that just gives you more knowledge. That doesn't help you become more conscious. That doesn't help you wake up. Find what is aware of those thoughts. Find what is aware of the gap between the thoughts. What's this that's aware? Now this is interesting. This is sky. This is your own true nature.

S: The next question is from Vijit.

V: Hello.

S: Okay. Lots of questions. But I'll just think of this moment and come up with what I'm feeling in this moment. Okay, so I feel better since I talked to you last week. I feel that yes, I have to start early. As soon as I wake up, do something with it. I've been working out as soon as I wake up and it gets better. I have this one question that sometimes, I do get present when I'm sitting, and my mind becomes clearer and this thing that you were talking about in the last question that you practise, I find that being attentive to your own breath sounds easy, but constantly being aware of your breath is a very hard task. Especially when things around you bring you back, drag you back to past or maybe towards the future or things that you're supposed to do in the day. And so my actual question is: how do you actually manifest something which you know is important for you, but still be not attached with the outcome? Let's just say I want to manifest in the coming few months, something that is valuable, and I need that thing?

V: Okay. So, say you want a glass of water and you want to manifest it. Well, you get up and you go to a tap and you pour yourself a glass of water into a glass that you found in a cupboard. That's how you do it. You make it so.

S: Yes. So, mind is constantly running, and when I bring my attention to my breath, then it's fine, but if I'm trying to manifest something, let's just say I have someone coming over and I need an internship. I need to make X amount of effort to get that. And I

know that, okay, resume, yes, that's the first thing, then applications, that's the second thing. You get rejections, you learn from them and then you update something in your work. Then again, reapply. I mean, that's very clear. That's how you get anything, especially if you want an internship or any job. But the thing is, when you actually keep on thinking, thinking in one direction, there comes a moment where your mind becomes burned out, and it just keeps on beating itself. After a certain point of that, what do I do now? You're just stuck, and that happens quite a lot. Often, I just don't know how to get around it.
V: Well, you started by talking about how tiring it is to keep watching the breath and it can be, but that's only because you've been living in your head for so long. To change that pattern is going to take a bit of discipline and that's what meditation is. It's a discipline which goes against the pattern of dreaming that you've been doing for a long time. To break that pattern in myself and get back in touch with reality, at the age of 34, I took my shoes off and walked around Australia for four years barefoot. I did that because I wanted to feel the earth under my feet. When we feel the earth under our feet, we're feeling something that is real. It is another way to meditate, because we're putting awareness on what is real. When you're barefoot, if you're not careful, you're going to hurt your feet, particularly walking around Australia. So it allowed me to practise being present to my feet and to my breath continuously for about four years, which allowed me to gain a great deal of present moment awareness.

S: Yes. So what I feel from your talk is that, yes, it is not an easy task. In the beginning, it does sound that putting your attention on one object is easy, but then after a certain point it becomes hard. These days, I'm feeling better, but the moment I talk to people, let's just say my parents, and they are still suffering, I feel like – especially when I talk to my mother – I feel like I take her thoughts into me after a certain point and that is distracting and I feel bad. I mean, I feel empathy, if that's what you want to call it, but I feel like it's very useless, and when I start empathising with people, it just kind of drags me down.

V: Yeah, because you're buying the story. You see, when people give you sad stories, that's just what it is: a sad story. It's not really a reality or a truth. People love sharing their misery, unfortunately, but you don't have to buy it. You can listen to it without buying it. If you buy it, if you go into it with them, you're lost in the dream just as much as they are. I can listen to people's sad stories without entering their dream. As a matter of fact, I never enter their dream because that's all it is. It's a dream. But once you enter it, then you get this very strong energy connection as well and it locks the energy of that – the person who's talking, which is probably some form of misery – into yourself.

S: Yes, when I talked to my mother, I listened to her because she's suffered a loss of a child. And that I understand, okay, that is something that no parent should witness, but unfortunately, that's how life is.

V: You're telling me a sad story right now and that's all it is, it's a sad story. If I was to go into it and start feeling the pain of it, I'm starting to produce that inside myself.

S: Yes, I see what you're saying.

V: Yeah, I'm not buying your story. I'm listening to you, but I'm not buying it because it's just a story. You're just making it up as you're going along. It's not happening now.

S: Yes.

V: Which means it's not real.

S: Yes, yes, that's true. I feel like when I talk to my mother, she wants me to validate her thoughts. If I don't validate, then she becomes defensive.

V: You can validate her.

S: I want to help her, but if I try to do that, it becomes trickier.

V: No, no, you can validate her. You don't have to believe it though. You know, you can have compassion for your mother. You can see that she's suffering. You can validate her story without buying one bit of it. And you're doing that out of empathy for her. She's already lost, but the moment you buy it, you're also lost.

S: So one thing I noticed in myself is that when I'm present, I feel good. I know I can manifest something, I want to do something, it's a fresh energy. But when I listen to people around me, everyone having their sad story, when they start talking there is something in me that goes "I want to help this person, I want to do something about it" and the moment I've tried doing that, I just realise I have become them and lost myself in that.

V: How can you help? How can you help people if you're just as lost as they are? The moment you buy the story you're just as lost they are.

S: I think I'm absolutely lost in their story. And it's my mind's way of telling me, okay, you can do this. That's fine. You're fine right now, but this person is suffering. You can do something.

V: No no, you're dreaming. You're dreaming. You've gone into a dream and you're believing it. You're lost and nothing's happening. It's just a story, but you're lost in a dream the same as the person who's telling you the story is lost in a dream. Now there are two lost people.

S: Yes, so right.

V: I need to talk to you about this. Look, I worked as a psychotherapist for nearly 10 years and I got constant sad stories because that's why people come to psychotherapists, because they're unhappy. They come because they're lost. They're in pain. They don't know their way out, right? Now, if I had bought their sad stories, I'm just as lost as they are. Yes. How can I help them then?

S: So there is this thing where I know what you're saying, but when I . . . when I listen to anyone, I actually attentively listen to them. I can almost feel, okay, that's where they're stuck. But if I try to input anything in, and I say, "Hey, this is not helping you one bit," the moment I say something like that, especially my mother, she becomes defensive.

V: I don't understand why you'd want to do that.

S: So you're just saying when someone is telling their

story, you just keep on listening to it and don't have to really give your input in that.

V: You can just acknowledge that you've heard them because people love to be heard and when they feel they're not heard, they get hurt. So someone's telling you a sad story. You can say, "Yeah, I've heard you, I hear you" – something like that so they feel heard. You're not necessarily agreeing with them. You're not entering the story. You're just saying that you've listened.

S: Right. Yes, I feel like this old pattern in me of trying to help people is almost like a trap in my head because I'm mostly attracting people who are suffering around me these days.

V: The whole world is suffering. Don't worry, everyone's got a sad story because everyone's on a cross somewhere, but you don't have to buy it. You don't have to get caught in the dream if you don't want to. You're choosing to get caught in the dream and then you're justifying being caught in the dream.

S: Interesting. Yes, I guess I'm going to practise more what I'm constantly doing. I feel comfortable in that. I feel when I go to sleep, I'm constantly aware of my breath. And I see myself dreaming. I mean, the thoughts come inside my head, and I can almost see them. When I lose awareness of my breath, I have started dreaming and it happens in like a split second. Last night, I went and lay down on the ground, right next to my bed, and within 10 seconds I was dreaming. I saw my ex in my dream and she was talking to me. Where did she come from? And I wasn't even thinking about her throughout the day. My mind has a lot of intensity with it. It's not easy to deal with it. It feels like a lot of pressure. It's a constant awareness.

V: Whatever you practise you'll get good at. If all you practise is dreaming, which is what most adults practise, that's all you're ever good at. If you practise present moment awareness to what is real, you get good at it, but only because you practise it.

S: Yes. Yes, that makes sense. Thank you, Vishrant. I think today I don't have more complaining questions.

V: I hear a lot of suffering. People suffer. They do suffer, but it doesn't help, really, to be a victim of it ever, because that just creates more suffering.

S: Yes, so I have to take responsibility that, okay, even if someone else is suffering, I have to take responsibility. I don't need to suffer. I can just listen to them.

V: Don't buy the dream. They're just dreaming at you. And they're telling you their dream. You don't have to buy it because it's not actually happening right now anyway. If it's happening right now, you can do something physically about it, but it's not happening right now. It's a dream. It's not real.

S: But sometimes I feel like when I listen to people, I can almost see that they are creating their suffering and I do that many times.

V: Yeah, you do.

S: When something terrible happens in their life, I almost feel that if they were to know that they are creating this suffering, and that this event that happened in their life is actually the manifestation of their old habits, it brings their aggression, and people get crazy because they just realised that they have been wasting so much time of their life.

V: I think our conversation has come to an end today.

S: Yeah, I understand. I'll come with something better.

V: Nice to talk to you.

S: Nice talking to you Vishrant as well.

~

V: Hello Sarah.

S: Hi Vishrant. I've been practising observing the breath, but with that, also, the mantra of "I am": "I" on the in-breath, and "am" on the out-breath. Would you say that this is more or less beneficial than just observing the breath?

V: Look, I never really supported that particular methodology. I'm not saying that it doesn't work. It may work. It's just not something that I found worked for me. So I only teach people what worked for me because I know it works. I don't know if the "I am" on the in- and out-breath works. I just don't know. I'm not into entertaining the mind and I would find that entertaining the mind because you're using the mind to say "I," then you're using the mind to say "am". I'd rather not use the mind at all. I'd rather just witness the whole thing. So you're witnessing the breath coming in. You're witnessing the breath going out. You're just witnessing. You're not doing anything else. You add the "I" and "am" and you're doing something. I'm not in favour of doing anything.

Witnessing works. The only thing that I am in favour of is self-inquiry. Who's aware of the breath? Who's aware of this? That I advocate. But look, it may work, it's just not my experience.

S: Sure, yeah, I wondered that because you know, the breath being real, yet you're actually applying thought to it. That was the confusion there.

V: Yes, that's what I said.

S: But I have found that it's somewhat quicker to identify thought when it comes in by applying the "I am".

V: I used to just watch the breath. And I found that that works. And thought comes in, you discount the thought and come back to the breath. I don't think anyone has ever said learning this stuff is easy, because it's not.

S: No.

V: It would have been easier for us to learn it when we were children, before we went to school, because we're already very present then. But after we've been to school for 12 years or however many years, we're very entrenched in dream. Is there anything else?

S: No, thank you.

V: Nice to talk to you.

~

V: Hello, Angel.

S: Hello. Vishrant, how do we listen and tune into you?

V: So the words affect the mind because they mean something and there's an understanding that happens in the brain, but under the words there's a current, and this current is the current that is created when awareness is aware of itself in a human being, commonly called a Buddha field. Now, whenever someone who's awake talks, there is this undercurrent of energy in the words and so you can tune in to that energy field and you're starting to tune into something that will expand your mind, open your Heart and give you clarity, and has the potential of even waking you up. The words themselves don't do much. They're just knowledge really and knowledge is the booby prize in the game of higher consciousness. Tune into the energy field. Let it take you. Surrender to it. Die in it. Find yourself as it. In that energy field, it is easier for awareness to find itself. Just let go. Let go. Let go.

I found myself – in the energy field of my teachers – as the universe. What they were saying wasn't important. The energy field they were carrying, the Buddha field – that was important. That is satsang. You can collect knowledge by going to a library. Most libraries have all of the old masters' works. It doesn't help. What helps, really helps, is being in the presence of someone who's awake. Satsang.

Thank you for satsang. Good to see you bravehearts here today.

CHAPTER EIGHT

The Recipe for Success in Spirituality

V: Welcome to satsang.
S: Hello Vishrant. Can you please talk about the topic, the recipe for success in spirituality?
V: Okay. So I was very lucky, I was very fortunate that I came across mentors when I was 19 years old who trained me in how to be successful in the material world. Those mentors were working for an organisation called Focal Universal and Focal ran encounter groups they called the Greatness in You Seminars which were a four-day encounter group for having a look at yourself and taking yourself apart by removing limiting belief systems. But they also ran BMTs, business motivation training, and I'm not sure exactly how often they ran them, but it felt like it was monthly weekends and I did nine years of those. I loved it. I just loved learning about myself and other people, how things all worked in the world. I felt like I really began my education after I left school, rather than when I was at school. I practised what these teachers taught me, I put them into practice, and went into business, and by the age of 28 I'd retired. I didn't have to work anymore. I'd learnt the recipe for success and I applied it.

It turns out that the recipe for success in business, in sport, in music, in arts and in any endeavour you do, higher consciousness included, is all the same. It's not different. The first thing you do is you find somebody who knows the way, somebody who has higher consciousness, preferably someone who's enlightened, and you become their student. As a student, you listen to what they have to say and you follow their instruction because they know more than you. Unfortunately, Australian males, and females for that matter too, tend to like to think they know so they try doing things without advice, thinking that somehow even though they've never trained in it, they're going to be good at it – whether it's business or higher consciousness or anything else. Truth is, you get a mentor, someone who knows the way, and you learn from them. This is the beginning.

I was lucky enough to have mentors in business and mentors in personal growth. Then at the age of 28, about the time I retired, I got a spiritual mentor. His name was Bhagwan Shree Rajneesh. I listened to him and I followed his instructions. I already understood the recipe for success, but the beginning is always to get someone who knows the way to help you. Trying to do it by yourself is a waste of time. It's just arrogance actually, thinking you know something that you haven't ever been taught.

Now, along the way, I learned that totality is important. If you want to be successful at anything you have to be total, and if you are total, the chances are you're going to win, you're going to succeed. Totality is probably the most important part of any endeavour that we adventure on. How total you are or how partial you are at anything is going to determine your success or failure. All of the people who I know who were successful in business were total in what they were doing. The same goes for all of the people I know who have been successful at higher consciousness who were total in their endeavour to raise their consciousness levels. Totality rules the day. Now, if we look at what totality means, it means you have a disciplined mind. You have a mind that doesn't stop. You have a mind that doesn't give itself excuses for failure. As a matter of fact, any excuse for failure pretty much guarantees it. You have a mind that basically does what it says it's going to do. It doesn't stop. It doesn't give itself excuses to get out of anything. It makes it so. This is the totality that works in every endeavour in life if we want to succeed, including higher consciousness. So a disciplined mind sets a time to meditate every day and then makes it so. A disciplined mind doesn't give itself a choice. That is what discipline is: no choice. People who are flaky, people who give themselves choices to opt out don't make it. How can they? It's not going to happen. It's up to you what you do or what you don't do.

What became obvious to me in personal growth was that I had a heap of limiting belief systems that had been put into me by my parents, by my schooling, by my religion, by my government, and they needed to be changed. I started observing my mind quite closely when I was young and I recognised that these belief systems weren't actually real. They had just been programmed into me or brainwashed into me, so I started removing them. The first two that I challenged were worry and victim-orientated thinking. We think we need to worry, and victim-orientated thinking is often combined with worry. I started challenging my victim-orientated thoughts by looking at what happened when I became a victim. What belief systems was I holding when the expectation of those belief systems wasn't met and I became a victim and went into resistance of life, creating suffering for myself? I started removing those belief systems because I was not interested in volunteering to be a victim of life, of a person, of a thing, of a situation and hurting myself. People think other people hurt you. No, they don't. You hurt yourself. You hurt yourself, because you turn yourself into a victim. You volunteer to be a victim. Nobody's hurting anyone. People can do things that you don't like. People can do things that might hurt you physically, but you're the one who has to be a volunteer of it. I started to see life as "this is what is" rather than good-bad, right-wrong. This is simply what is. I stopped being a victim and my life improved immensely because I wasn't creating suffering for myself by going into resistance to everything that I didn't agree with. This is a part of the recipe for success in higher consciousness. Victim orientation is basically you not taking responsibility for how you feel because you make yourself feel. The world doesn't make you feel, you make yourself feel. This level of maturity doesn't really allow for higher consciousness. This level of maturity keeps you locked in lower consciousness. So it's up to you.

You're creating your reality by the way you think. It's all up to you.

My spiritual teacher Bhagwan Shree Rajneesh taught me how to meditate, taught me how to self-inquire, taught me how to practise the Way of the Heart, taught me how to accept life as it is – he taught me how to fly. I followed his instruction. I didn't arrogantly think that I knew better. I followed his instructions and this is the key. The key is really finding someone who is further ahead than you in whatever, and then following their instruction and following it to the letter. They've already proven that what they do works so when I used to listen to my teachers, I had an attitude. I listened to them like my life depended upon it because it did.

Are there any questions, any statements, any challenges to anything that's been said here today?

S: The first question is: Does having a nice and loving personality have anything to do with success in spirituality?

V: Depends on whether that personality is just selling out to get along or whether it's actually genuine. If you sell out to get along, you're not gonna get too far. You've got to stand your ground. In business, success demands that you stand alone in resistance. In higher consciousness, it demands that you stand alone in surrender. People who sell out to get along, to get the acceptance of others, twist themselves into knots that are so false it's not funny, just so they can be accepted by others. This is one of the things that needs to be removed, and when you look at why people look for acceptance outside of themselves, it's usually because they're not accepting themselves. Somewhere inside they don't feel worthy. Somewhere inside, they just don't feel enough. That comes down to the basis or the beginning, the foundation of higher consciousness, which is self-acceptance. Do you accept every part of you? Are you able to hold every part of your psyche in tenderness? Or are there parts that you're judging heavily, beating yourself up over, creating a separation in your own mind as a result between the part that's judging and the part that's probably now hiding. Self-acceptance is the foundation for higher consciousness.

S: Next, we have a question from Mihir.

V: Hello.

S: Hey, Vishrant. My question was slightly unrelated to the topic. I've been using weed in my life as a reward system and when I don't use it, I feel like I'm very unmotivated and I feel like there's no point in doing all the work. Also, my parents are very unaccepting of it and judge me for it, but the periods I have gone like four or five months without it, I feel like they're very dull. Do you have any advice?

V: What do you use as a reward system? I missed the word.

S: Marijuana.

V: Marijuana as a reward system, that's a good one. Okay, I do understand marijuana and how it works and why it works and what it does for you. Unfortunately, they call it dope for a reason, because it actually takes you into dreamland. Marijuana, like opiates, is a dream drug. It takes you into a dream zone which is relaxing. That's why you like it because it feels good, but it takes you further into lower consciousness. It doesn't take you into higher consciousness. If you're actually into higher consciousness, any drug that takes you into dreamland – like marijuana or an opiate – is in the way. It's actually headed in the wrong direction which is a shame but it's the truth. Yes, marijuana relaxes you, but it takes you into a dream world, takes you into lower consciousness, and it doesn't take you into higher consciousness. So I can't support people using drugs that take them into lower consciousness if they're interested in higher consciousness.

Of course, if they're not interested in higher consciousness I really don't mind. When students come along and they want to go to higher consciousness, I can't endorse the taking of marijuana or opiate drugs, because I know what they do. They just take you into dreamland. They take you further away from higher consciousness. So it sounds like the way you're using marijuana is as a medication, probably to relax you. Probably to make you feel better in the tension of the world that you live in, but it's definitely not going to raise your consciousness levels. It's going to lower them, I'm afraid.

~

S: The next question is from Marcus.
V: Hey, Marcus.
S: Hi. So I had a realisation today and I would like to get your view on it. The realisation was that this

whole time I've been trying to change something about myself, which was all of these thoughts in the background throughout the day, and I realised that it's not about changing that to no thoughts, it's about accepting that those thoughts are there.

V: Okay. So do you want an opinion on that?

S: Yeah.

V: Okay. Acceptance is great. Witnessing the mind and seeing what the mind is up to is also great. As a matter of fact, it's where we begin because if we don't see what's going on, we're really in the dark. So you develop this witness, it just witnesses the mind, but some of the things that you see – because you remember what's been witnessed – some of the things you see are obviously detrimental to you and possibly to others. So those things, you can change. You can accept that they're there. There's no problem with that. That's the first thing you need to do, accept what's there. If they're detrimental to you, then it's not a bad idea to change them.

What I saw when I was very young was that I was a victim-orientated thinker which I inherited from mum and it was detrimental to me. It wasn't doing me any favours. It was creating suffering in me. So I changed it. That took a couple of years. It didn't happen overnight. I had to stop supporting victim-orientated thinking and I had to start removing belief systems that created victim-orientated thinking. I think that was one of the best things I ever did for myself ever. I started doing that when I was 19 and by the age of 21 I wasn't victim-orientated thinking anymore. I just look back at all of the years I didn't suffer as a victim as a result of changing that, that way of thinking. I did move to change, but I accepted it first. If I failed, I accepted that too and I'd try it again. Acceptance is really important, but if you notice something that's detrimental happening inside you, why would you leave it there?

S: I've realised that by watching my mind, I'm very competitive, even, like unconsciously competitive, and I want to know how to change that.

V: Well, we all are competitive because we went to school and we got taught how to compete with people to get better marks, be better at sport, be better at this, be better at that, art, whatever. We were trained to be competitive, which is about as ugly as you can get really, because what it did effectively is created so much low self-worth in kids who weren't making the grade, because someone was beating them. It just wounded the hell out of our children and we still do it to this day. We put them in an environment that is highly competitive, teach them how to be little soldiers, you know, so they can go off and fight one day. This is why I homeschooled my children. I wasn't interested in putting them into a competitive environment where they learned how to win at the cost of others. Look at it. Study it yourself. You study what is competition, understand it completely that competition itself is about as ugly as you can get and it's against the Heart. It's against love because when you're truly in touch with love, you don't want to beat someone, you don't want to make them feel less-than by beating them. You actually want them to be your friend. So you want to play a game where everyone wins.

S: That means no more chess?

V: Well look, if you want to get a degree, you have to pass the tests. If you want to get a diploma on the wall, you have to pass the tests. But you've got to look at it inside of yourself. Look at it, what it does to you and what it does to others, when you win and someone loses or when they win and you lose. How beautiful is that or how ugly is that? This is the schooling system we were involved in. It just damages children.

S: That was a great answer. There's one more question. I have so many dreams every night. In the morning, I have an alarm. I snooze it, that goes on for an hour, where I'm just in bed, like half dreaming and half awake, but I want to be able to just snap into reality. At the very beginning of the day, how would you recommend I do that?

V: Okay, I understand the question. What I did to overcome that is, you wake up too early in the morning and go "Ah, it's too early, I'll stay in bed" and then you go into another dream stage. So what I did is any time that I woke up, even if it was too early, I'd get out of bed. I'd get out of bed and I'd make my bed because when you get out of bed and you make your bed, you're moving into doing something that's real. It takes you right out of dream. If you get out of bed and just sleep walk to the bathroom, well, you're still dreaming, but if you get out of bed and you make your bed, the act of making the bed takes you out of dream and that becomes a habit. But it becomes a habit because you make sure you do it every time. You've got a habit and the habit is to stay in bed and dream. To break that habit, you have to do something different than what you've been doing and the something different is that you wake up, get out of bed and make your bed.

S: Okay, how about because I have a partner when I wake up, I don't want to disturb her. So I was wondering if I can do something different, like you know, I have an electric kettle so I could just like pour some water and just start warming up my water would that work too?

V: Well, you could get dressed or have a shower. I mean anything that you have to do in the real world will take you out of dream. I suggest making the bed, but if there's someone still in the bed that's a bad idea. You've got to roll them out and make the bed, right? No, that doesn't work so well. No, you get out of bed yourself and you go and have a shower or whatever you do in the mornings. Get dressed. As soon as you move to doing something physically that takes a little bit of effort, you're moving back into reality.

S: Okay, yeah because even in the shower, it's very hard for me to come out of the dream so what I started doing –

V: Where do you live or where are you from?

S: Boston, Massachusetts.

V: Ah yes, it gets nice and cold up there in the winter. See, if you get in that shower and you turn the hot shower on you have a hot shower then suddenly you turn it off you turn the cold on, I'll bet you'll get present really quick. Extremely quick. You'll be so present and so fresh it won't be funny. But you've got to fool yourself. You've got to fool yourself. You've got to pretend you're not doing it while doing it. You turn the hot off and you turn the cold on and then you stand there and scream a bit.

S: Screaming. A lot of screaming.

V: Well, it definitely brings you to clarity.

S: That's right. I'll start implementing that.

V: Yeah, you try to keep continuing to dream in Boston when you turn the cold on in winter. I bet you can't.

S: Correct. Now what about the reverse? What about going to sleep having all of those thoughts when I'm trying to go to sleep?

V: Okay, so when I'm telling you these things, I'm telling you things I used to use. I'm not telling you abstract ideas. These are the things I used to use. I like being fresh in the morning. So if I get up, I would have a cold shower after a hot shower and it would just freshen me up for the whole day. It would be a great start. As far as going to sleep at night, I found that if I tried to go to sleep when I couldn't go to sleep, it just caused pressure. So what I did is I just allowed myself to stay awake and eventually, because I wasn't putting any pressure on myself to go to sleep, I'd eventually go to sleep. I just made it okay not to sleep. So I just lay there with my eyes open or my eyes shut and I'd stay in bed in the acceptance that

sleep wasn't there just yet. There was no resistance to it, in other words. Actually, it's the resistance to it that keeps us awake.
S: I gotcha.
V: Because we're tired. We want to go to sleep. We can't. But we're pressuring ourselves to go to sleep. That resistance keeps us awake.
S: Beautiful. Thank you Vishrant.

~

S: Hi Vishrant, it's Indrapal. So it's such a pleasure speaking with you. It's unbelievable. I did your session that you just last had and now this one and can't believe I'm actually talking to you.

My question is this: deep in meditation, you know, there are definitely times when I have had flickers/glimpses of getting to a place where the mind is really silent, and having almost the perception of myself just becoming part of the aether, just not in my body. And so that in and of itself has been phenomenal in a way because I was there, but I wasn't in my body, in my physical body. Having said that, you know, you've talked a little bit today about following instruction and having a mentor so is there a simplified way of knowing or measuring our progress? Where are we on this path? And so where do we start off with a road marker if you kind of understand the gist of my question?
V: I can give you the road marker straight up. When I was 28, I started meditating under the instruction of my master and I found no-mind. Now, sitting in no-mind, which is what you're talking about, I got to see that I was there, but the mind wasn't there. I

got to see that there was no thinking, but I was still there, which brought about the question in my mind, who am I really? Because up to that point, I believed I was the mind and I was the body. Then all of a sudden I'm sitting in no-mind, there's nothing here, and then later, the mind comes and goes. It remembers I was there, but there was nobody there. There were no thoughts, not a thought, but I was still there. So if I'm not my thoughts, what am I really? And that's the beginning. That's the marker. So you've already hit that point. Now the quest is to find out what is it that's there, that's always there. Actually, even when the mind is talking, it's still there. What is this that is simply there and is aware? That's when my quest for Enlightenment began when I realised that I wasn't the mind, that I could be here without thoughts. What am I really? Who am I really? The curiosity got to me and of course the curiosity killed the cat.

S: Yes, certainly, and this happened to me very recently, a few weeks ago, weekends ago, and so that weekend was really somewhat of a daze because I very heavily had that feeling of no-mind and not being in my body. And overall, you know, with work and following Osho's teachings, I have looked at my triggers and my patterns and I still have some highly-resistant patterns that I'm working with, trying to be a witness to and looking at those things. Just observing, witnessing them, not really trying to suppress, but –

V: What you're talking about now is what led to the first awakening, and the first awakening happened for me in 1987, two years after chatting with Osho.

He blew my mind and two years after chatting with him, I'd been involved in groups called enlightenment intensives, which were seven-day and 14-day groups where you just ask the question "Who am I?" to a partner. It would be answered. The answer would be discounted, then the same question asked back to you. And I was doing this on the foreshore, walking along the river by myself. I'd been walking from six in the morning and it was about 10 o'clock when the first satori began. I was so relaxed in asking the question and then discounting it – that's a Zen methodology of self-inquiry – the witness that was witnessing me asking the question became me. I was it, and then I became the universe. No "I" any longer, just the universe, using Osho's methodology of self-inquiry, while witnessing the self-inquiry. By myself, my mind was relaxed. I wasn't trying to get anything. I wasn't trying to get anywhere. I was absolutely relaxed. I was prepared to self-inquire all day long. I was just doing it for fun while I was walking along the river. It changed my life, because now I knew what I was. I came back to ego-based reality, but now I knew what I was and I knew I wasn't the body and I knew I wasn't a mind. I knew that the body and mind was simply a spacesuit, which that that I was, pure awareness, was using to be here.

S: Okay, okay, and then did it stick, after that experience you had? That was it, then you basically had reached, per se?

V: I had, but I came back to ego-based reality. Some of its stuck, but I didn't know, I wasn't aware of that at the time. My third eye opened, my crown chakra opened, my throat was already open, my Heart was kind of semi-open, but not open enough. The crown stayed, the third eye stayed, and it gave me a sense of being everything. At that time, I didn't realise that was satori because I was still looking for the wham-bam-thank-you-ma'am satori where I was the universe – the Buddha on the path, in other words – so I didn't recognise that I was in satori, in a milder form of satori. That went on for the next 11 years and I hadn't recognised what it was. It was only later in hindsight that I saw there was something there the whole time, and I was missing it. My mind was missing it because I was looking for something bigger. Then I went to an Advaita Vedanta meeting with a guy called Isaac Shapiro and I was quite sceptical of him, but I went into the meeting anyway, down in Denmark, which is south of Perth in Western Australia. And the moment he walked in the door, I woke up again. I became the universe again, every particle being love. Now that went away as well, but for the next year, I had a thousand satoris. Then in another retreat with another awake teacher, I found myself as Truth and it has been like that ever since, 23 years now. There's no sense of somebody being here, but there is a sense of being everything at once and nothing, if that makes sense. My mind flatlined about 22 to 23 years ago. My mind flatlined.

S: Wow, and I know what you're describing and I'm hesitant because I have doubt with my mind. Just because this is relatively new for me, but definitely

I felt like I was everything all at once, but not tangibly, you know, in that experience and so ... so you're saying in retrospect too, it seems like you had that experience, you recognised it only down the line, but subsequently, you had multiple such experiences. So I guess I wouldn't say that it was stuttering, but it came and went, came and went, and perhaps obviously, the frequency for you increased. Do we just keep doing what we're doing then? Or do I just keep doing what I was doing because when this happened to me, I was doing a meditation retreat, semi-retreat, half-day kind of thing. We started off with one of Osho's chakra meditations, then we went into his death meditation. And then it was the very first time that I had done the "Who am I?" as well with Osho, you know, in his voice, and that is what resulted in that experience for me. And I'm not quite myself, I'm a physician in the worldly world so I'm very, very mind orientated, but over the last three, four years, I initially thought I had no Heart, but I've discovered I have a Heart, and much more Heart now. So suggestions for what to do as I keep hopefully progressing without being goal-orientated, I guess?

V: Okay, so what happened for me in the 12 months, where I had a thousand satoris, is I realised that awareness kept coming back to my mind because I kept contracting every now and again over things that weren't working in my life, and I got to realise that these things that I was contracting on were obstacles in the way of Enlightenment. Anything that creates a contraction in you, anything that creates resistance in you can attract awareness back to the mind, away from itself. When you're awake, awareness is aware of itself, the witness is aware of itself. And in the beginning, in the early days, I think that's a fragile position. The mind needs to support what has been found because if it contracts and goes into resistance, awareness, even if it's on itself, in the early days, is likely to come back to the mind itself. The work, if you want to call it work, is to undo the mind to make it equanimous so it doesn't constantly get disturbed. Does that make sense?

S: Yes, yes, yes. And interestingly, it's been really poignant in the last week or two since this has happened. It's almost like you're suggesting, and my experience has been, that the mind itself seems to have some resistance. I think even after this, it's interesting. I have resistance in terms of the points where I contract my triggers. For the most part prior to this, I was a little more mellow. I don't know if it's weird, minding now, because I had that experience. And I'm not talking like "Oh, my gosh, I had that experience and I achieved some major thing". It's almost like I'm afraid and I want to downplay it on some level, and just be like, "Okay, that's good. Just carry on". But because that happened, I feel like my mind is being harder on itself, like when I get triggered, or if I go into a mind pattern or something. I guess I just need to get back to like, what you're saying: just undo the mind and really work hard again.

V: I'm using the term "work hard," but be aware of that and just relax back into it.

Okay, so when you had the satori, it's like an invitation. It's an invitation to come home because Beingness is home. It's what we really are. You've received the information, now you need to do the work to get everything out of the way so you can come home, but you're a doctor, which means you have a professional persona. Now in that professional persona, I'll bet that you don't contract too much because you remain professional. Now extend that professional persona to every part of your life. It's not personal anymore.

S: Wow, okay.

V: That's actually what I did. After I got out of publishing and walked around Australia for four years, I went back to school and trained as a psychotherapist and a naturopath. And one day, I just realised that when I was with my clients, there was none of me there, there was no story of Vishrant there, I was just there for my clients. I realised that was very peaceful. It was really nice just to be there for someone else and not there with my trippy story, so I extended that to my whole life. I got rid of the story of Vishrant, the story of contraction, the story of resistance.

S: Okay, thank you. I think that's a great place. I think that's something tangible that I can definitely –

V: Well, you already have the professional persona, so you've just got to extend it outside your work.

S: Okay, okay, so I will do that. Thank you very much.

V: Look, you're very, very welcome. And I love what's happening for you, I really do. Keep in touch.

S: I certainly will, thank you.

S: The next question has been written by Brian: You say that silence is the highest teaching. Is this the silence that is found when we rest in the still and empty background in which the mind appears?

V: It is, but there needs to be an understanding of what I'm talking about. Someone who is ready, is ready for silence, they don't need a teacher to say anything. They may need the presence of the teacher, but they don't need a teacher to say anything anymore. Mouna teachers, which means silent teachers, are enough. For most people, they need a teacher who talks so they can understand how to allay the mind. Silence is the highest teaching, but only those who are ready for silence are ready for a silent teacher. They are the ones who have already mastered their own mind and learnt surrender.

S: The next question has been written by Robert: I'm a seeker of the Truth. How can you help me to be enlightened?

V: Robert, Robert, Robert, Robert, Robert. I remember what Osho said. He said, "I'm not your dear old uncle, I'm here to murder you". How can I help you Robert? If you're a student of mine, my intention would be to help you die as an "I" so you can know yourself as your true nature, but you're not a student of mine so I can't help you a great deal. I suggest you find someone who's awake and go and hang out with them and I know what their job is. It's the same as my job: to help people learn to die so they can find themselves as Truth.

S: The next question has been written by Narrateme: I was diagnosed with cancer in 2017. I've heard Osho say that cancer is a blessing. I see how any moment the body can cease to be. There is apprehension about the unknown, but I remain with the witness. Although there is some fear, I stay with awareness. Can you please comment?

V: Yeah. You need to be willing to die. It's that simple. You see, the reason Osho said that is a blessing is because he understands that it's an opportunity for surrender. Unconditional surrender to the inevitability of the loss of life. That opportunity, if taken, puts you in the right place for Enlightenment. Unconditional surrender is something the mind needs to learn. And it learns through practice. Because you have cancer, you can practise over and over again until you master the mind and become absolutely okay with death.

~

S: Hey Vishrant, I was just asking how do I deal with my parents trying to control my behaviour and always judging me for what I'm doing? They're not accepting of it. This is regarding the marijuana and they always think of it in a negative light and it makes me feel really guilty as well in doing it.

V: How old are you?

S: 22.

V: Move out of the house. You're 22 years old, man. You know, your mummy and daddy are still telling you what to do. I'm sorry, but you've put yourself in the line of fire. Now you either wear it or you don't, you know. If I was you, I wouldn't be hanging around my parents. Of course, they're going to give you a hard time. They've got judgments about it. They think it's a stepping stone to maybe a heavier drug, you know, like a gateway drug to heroin or something. They've got all of their fears running. They want the best for you so of course they're going to give you a hard time. But you are responsible for being there. You've put yourself in the line of fire and you're copping it. And you're wanting to know how to stop it. Get out of there.

If you were 16 or 17, or maybe even 18 I'd have a different story. But you're not. You're 22, man. You're old enough to be married and have kids.

S: Yeah.

V: The problem with marijuana is it demotivates you so there might not be much motivation for getting out there and getting your own place. It's a demotivating drug. It makes you feel relaxed, but it kills motivation, doesn't it?

S: Yeah, yeah, I feel like it, like when I'm using it. I don't try and use it and then do something that requires motivation. I use it as a reward system and yeah, that's if I don't use it in that way, I just feel unmotivated all of the time.

V: Yeah, look. What's the bet you're addicted to it? What's the bet the story that you're telling yourself about a reward system is just your addiction hiding? What's the bet? I think 100 per cent.

It's good to be honest with yourself, but unfortunately the addicted part of the mind is rarely honest because it wants what it wants and it doesn't care how it gets it. The addicted part of the mind can't really be trusted to tell the truth about anything. One of the first things you learn when you train as an addiction counsellor, and I did, is that addicts don't tell the truth, and you know it's true. You know it's true, because the addicted part of the mind does whatever it can to get whatever it wants.

S: Yeah.

V: Now if you want to have some peace from your parents, move out or give up dope, your choice. Stop blaming them for just being the way they are. They're just trying to take care of you, really. Make sense?

Their judgments about marijuana might be wrong, but so what? They're just trying to take care of you because they care about you, man.

S: Yeah.

V: Yeah.

S: Thank you.

V: Thank you. Nice chatting.

S: Yes, definitely.

~

S: Normally I come in with like, I'll try to think of a question beforehand and I didn't do that. So what the last guy was just saying, talking about, like the drug use and all that, like, I struggle with that same problem. And it's like, obviously in the way of waking up, because it's just one more thing for the mind to cling on to.

V: It's not just clinging. Marijuana makes you feel good. You know it does, it relaxes your mind. It makes you feel good. It takes you away from stress. It gives you release, relief. It's a medication. It's absolutely a medication and it works.

Unfortunately, it's in the way of higher consciousness because it takes you into dream. It's simple. What you're using works, but it demotivates you, takes you into the dream, and so there's a downside to it.
S: Yeah, so thanks for answering that, and like, you're definitely right about that. It's like it's . . . like the addictive part of the mind doesn't even want to acknowledge that it does take you into dream. Like, or to stop dreaming while you're doing those things.
V: Yeah, yeah, I used to smoke a bit of dope back in the late 80s and I found that the group of people I was hanging out with, they were always smoking dope. They'd have a puff of dope, the joint, a bong, whatever, and then chat about anything, you know, but everyone would be dreaming away. I realised the only way for me to get away from the drug was to actually get away from my friends because every time I saw them, they'd want you to have a smoke with them, you know? It was difficult. And I saw the light. I saw that, hey man, this is not raising my consciousness levels. This is demotivating me and it's keeping me lost in dream and it feels good. So that was the good bit, that it feels good. But the problem was, I was wasting my life dreaming. I was living in a dream, not in reality.
S: Yeah, so it's good to come back to reality. Right? Yeah. Thanks. Thanks for all that.
S: I wish you the best.

S: The next question is from Indrapal.

S: Hi Vishrant, it's me again. Actually, you can call me Indy. So just a few more things that popped into my mind.

V: What does Indrapal mean?

S: Indrapal? So Indra is the god of power, so it means that I have the power. So that's what that means, but I was born in England and basically as soon as Indiana Jones came out, Indrapal became Indy.

V: Ah, so Indrapal means power.

S: Yes.

V: Ah, I see. Okay. So, power. That's a cool name. We should put Prem in front of that. That would be powerful love.

S: Yeah, actually, that would have been good. It would have been good, you know, but I actually took sannyas last year, about a year ago in March of 2021. And my sannyas name is Prem Jyoti.

V: Joyti, what does Joyti mean?

S: Jyoti, Jyoti. J Y O T I. It means light.

V: Ah, the light of love?

S: Yes, yes.

V: Well, that's your path. Your path is love which is the Way of the Heart. That's a Heart name. That's definitely a Heart name, and being a doctor, you would be very good with the discipline, to some degree, but I believe in the marketplace it takes two wings to fly, not just the discipline, but also the Way of the Heart, love. And when we have both wings working we can fly high.

S: Absolutely. And I'm seeing glimpses of that as well. As I had said earlier, I joked with some of the sangha who I do meditation with, as I said before, I never thought I had a Heart. Extremely mind-orientated nature. On top of it, I'm an administrator, so I'm definitely all about "Get it done, get it done, get it done, this is the way it needs to be done, get it done". So it took me several years just to be able to start dropping that, and for the most part it's interesting. Well, it's because you are who you are, that you recognise some things that, you know, in a workplace, it's easy, easier to drop things than it is when we personalise things for ourselves. So yeah, my sensitivity and my Heart has definitely, definitely increased to a large degree.

V: Would you like it to increase more? I can tell you how.

S: Oh, absolutely, please.

V: Okay. So openness counts for everything because it's when we're open that we perceive love. When we're closed and defended, we cut ourselves off from it. And all of the defence systems are in the way. They're obstacles in the way of the Heart.

Yeah. So I started to find Heart and I was a businessman. I owned a publishing company that had 35 staff members and it was really go-go-go the whole time. Even though I had retired, I was still overseeing to some degree, and I started to find Heart and I realised that my business and the way I behaved in my business had a lot of closures in it, a lot of defences in it. I had 30-odd professional salesmen working for me who always try to take you, you know, do something weird, so I walked into my companies when I was 33 years old and I gave my multimillion-dollar company to my staff and walked out.

S: I read that about you how you ... wow.

V: Yeah.

S: That's guts.

V: I knew the recipe for success. I always thought that I could start again in something if I wanted to. You say it's guts, but I also had a lot of confidence in myself. I took my shoes off and I walked around Australia to find my Heart and to get back to reality. And I walked around for four years basically as a bum having the time of my life because I didn't have to be a somebody. As a publisher, I was a big somebody. I drove a Rolls Royce and lived in a penthouse in an expensive suburb. I had chauffeurs and I had cooks. I had everything. It was just lovely to get back to reality where nobody knew me, walking around Australia as a bum. The best, the very best time of my life was being a nobody going nowhere. And then I realised –

S: Sounds so good to be a nobody, anonymous, just nobody.

V: Absolutely, but then I found my Heart and my Heart affected my mind in such a way that I just wanted to help people, and I realised that all I was good at was business. So I went back to school and trained as a psychotherapist and naturopath to have the tools to be able to serve people.

S: I love that story because the profession I'm in has been very rewarding in the worldly sense, you know, but frankly it's become empty over time. I have been told – and I recognise it to some degree in myself – that I'm good with people and I think I have some innate naturally-given ability to be able to talk with people, at least with the casual feedback I get that people have enjoyed talking with me. I would love to do kind of similar to your path, not that I'm emulating your path by any means, but have had those sorts of thoughts, like, "Man, I wish I could just drop everything". My kids – one's in college and one's in high school still – so you know, I have a few things that I have to accomplish before I can kind of let go and maybe become a bum somewhere.

V: Do you work in a hospital or do you work in a private practice?

S: I actually work for the prison system.

V: Okay.

S: In California.

V: I can I talk to you about that. We are pushed to rush, hurry, hurry, hurry, get it done, get it done, get it done. We're pushed and pushed and pushed, and as a result, we lose the feel of service. If we really want to be in service, we have to give people time. We have to listen to them. We have to stop the rush, rush, rush, even if it costs some people not seeing us. At least the people who do see us are getting service. Does that make sense?

S: Right, oh absolutely, those are the most rewarding times when I've been able to do that.

V: You get better results because people need to be heard and when you're listening to them deeply, they feel loved as well.

S: And I'm feeling that too. I've noticed my sensitivity has increased. I can feel the . . . I mean, I don't know technically how you feel energy . . . but I feel that energy back from people when I have those kinds of interactions with them.

V: I used to book as a psychotherapist. I'd book an hour-long session. As a naturopath, I only did 20-minute sessions, but during those 20 minutes, they got the totality of me. During that hour, they got the totality of me. There wasn't a rush to get rid of anyone. I would listen and listen and listen because that's service. If we're rushing, we're in service to the prison system, not in service to the people we're actually serving, and there's a difference. The people we're serving are humans. The prison system is just an organisation.

S: I hear you. I hear you. I absolutely hear you. And yes, yes.

Somewhat more of a technical question now. When I first became involved with Osho, my first real exposure to meditation, and it's always been with Osho, happened in April of 2020. I did a series of meditations at that time and then did spend some time, about three months doing Nadabrahma meditation and dynamic or Kundalini, and that was very helpful. As you know, there's multiple stages, and the last part, which is sitting in silence, I found that I can sit in silence and can actually have moments of no thought and that's fine. Would you recommend doing any formal meditations anywhere? Is there a role of continuing to do Kundalini or any of those kinds of things or is sitting in silence as part of – you know, my daily practice sitting in silence is something I do – anything else on a more formal level that you would suggest doing?

V: Look, it depends where you're at on the path. Everyone wants to be further ahead than where they are. That's just human nature. But wherever you are, sitting silently is wonderful if you can stay with reality. Most people can't sit silently and stay with reality. They start dreaming. Nadabrahma is a beautiful meditation. I used to run the Nadabrahma classes at the Rajneesh Centre in Fremantle when I was a sannyasin down there and I just loved it, just beautiful. But whatever works for you.

So for the first 10 years of meditation, I used to love to watch my breath, and I'd sit in a half lotus position and watch my breath, but I'd keep my eyes open at a 45-degree angle so I wouldn't go into dream. The problem is dreaming. You see, when you're dreaming, when you're thinking, you're not in meditation. Your awareness is on thoughts. That's not meditation. Meditation is when your awareness is on what is real. I'm in meditation all of the time now because my awareness is on what is real, all of the time. My mind is flatlined. But when I walked around Australia to get back to reality, to get back to meditation, I took my shoes off so I could feel my feet because when you can feel your feet, you're actually meditating because you're with something that's real. I used to do walking meditation which is watching the breath and feeling your feet. Now, if you're watching your breath and feeling your feet, you can't think. If you do, you're going to lose it. You're going to lose touch with reality.

As a doctor, you will have been trained to live in your head for sure, so now it's time to reclaim reality from the dream that you found yourself in. The matrix of your own mind is now a prison. You can get out of it by practising something that's real, getting out of your head and into reality, and that is meditation. If you're aware of the sounds around you, you're in meditation. If you're aware of the sights and the sounds, you are in meditation. It's only what you think that is not meditation. That's dream.

S: Got it, got it. And I'm sorry I'm taking up so much time. Music. Is there a role of music? My sensitivity to music and being able, you know ... what is the role of music in this process? I can get very deeply into music, but I don't know, is that a dream, is that ... I'm not sure necessarily what I'm asking you?

V: Music can take you into the present moment because it's real. You're listening to it, but what I used to like to do with music was dance, and I'd throw my totality into the dance, and what that helped me do was clear my energy because I used to pick up a lot of energy from my clients in psychotherapy and naturopathy. I'd pick up a lot of density and it used to cloud my mind. So after work, I used to dance, and I'd really put my totality into the dance because I love to dance, and it just cleared my energy. It threw everything out. And so, music to me has always been a dancing phenomenon.

Look, I must go. It's way past time. I've got people ringing me telling me it's time.
S: Okay. Well, thank you very much for your guidance.
V: It was nice talking to you, it really is. Do keep in touch.
S: Certainly. Thank you.
V: Thank you for satsang. Good to see bravehearts here today.

CHAPTER NINE

What Are Energy-Clearing Practices?

V: Welcome to satsang.
S: Hello Vishrant. Can you please talk about what are energy-clearing practices?
V: When I was quite young, I got to understand that clarity is very important – to be able to see things clearly. I think I was about 16 or 17 years old when I realised that to have clarity, to be pristine, is a tremendous advantage in the world. It also is a tremendous advantage in the spiritual world.

During the day, we produce energy with the way we think. We also pick up energy from different people that we have the company of, and if we don't clear that energy, it can affect the way we think and it can ruin our clarity. So it's important – if you're interested in higher consciousness – to have clarity. Practices that help you clear energy you may have produced yourself or picked up from other people are important. You hang out with people who are dense because they've been grinding their minds, and you're emptier, you will take it on. Energy flows from full to empty. It's no one's fault. It's just what is. If you decide to grind your mind, you will produce dense energy as well, tamasic and rajasic, and this energy will affect how you think. It'll also affect how you see things. It'll affect your clarity.

So I loved present-moment awareness. You see, if you're really present, you don't produce density. It's only when you're living in your mind that you produce energy that's tamasic or rajasic. Little kids up to about the age of three have pretty pristine energy because they're not grinding their minds yet. They're not living in their heads yet. They're present to what's happening around them so they're not producing the type of energy that can destroy clarity. Coming back to the moment, being present to what is real, takes you out of your head and into reality. This gives you clarity. This enables you to see clearly what's happening around you.

So I fell in love with the present moment when I was quite young because I liked the clarity that it gave. The other thing that I really fell in love with was water: the ocean and the river. I was fortunate enough to be brought up near the river. And so I was in the river as often as I could and I was in the ocean as often as I could because I found that any kind of water tended to make me feel energetically cleaner, and I'm sure it did. After a few years, I considered the ocean my mother, in that it helped clean me every day that I went into it. I became a diver. I used to love diving underwater. It took me so firmly into the moment, and the ocean itself is energetically taking everything away from you that's dense. Along with that, different sports, dancing, any kind of sport will do – anything that's physical will help you clear.

What doesn't help you clear up is sitting in front of a computer and thinking. Doesn't work. Nature is beautiful. It helps us have clarity. Water is great. So when I wasn't close to the river or I couldn't get to the ocean, I'd have a cold shower. That would wash away different densities I may have been carrying and give me my clarity back, a pristineness back.

And so it's up to you. I think first of all you need to notice the different energies, notice how you're affected by different energies, because how we think quite often is affected by the energy we're picking up from others or that we produced ourselves and is sitting in our bodies. It's important in higher consciousness to have clarity. So if you don't have a clearing practice and you are producing density, or you are picking it up from colleagues or partners or whoever else you're associating with and you don't clear, well, you've handicapped yourself pretty badly. Pristine clarity allows you to see everything. It allows you to see through your mind. It allows that witness of the mind to be there, to see everything. Clarity is so important. So, keeping yourself pristine is important also. It's up to you though. Nobody's going to do it for you, and more than likely, no one will even tell you about it.

I had to work all this out by myself. I liked the idea of being successful in the world when I was young and I saw clearly that clarity made the difference between failure and success. So I got into clearing practices when I was quite young. It just turns out that those very same practices were great for higher consciousness and great for enlightenment. How pristine you are or how messy are you energetically is going to make a big difference in your life.

Are there any questions, any statements, any challenges to these teachings today?

S: The first question is: How can I tell within myself if I need to clear my energy field?

V: Well, are you feeling bright? Are you feeling switched on? Or are you feeling dull? Check and see. Check and see now. How're you feeling right now? What's the feeling? Are you feeling clear or are you feeling cloudy? Are you feeling up and bright or are you feeling dull and dim? Have a look and see because more than likely the energy you're carrying or not carrying is affecting how you feel.

S: Are auras real? And can you see them on people?

V: I have no interest in auras whatsoever. I don't look for them whether they're real or not. Someone who's awake has a presence. There's a light around them. I just don't have an interest in the subject.

S: The next question is from Abhayi.

V: Hello, Abhayi.

S: Hi Vishrant. Vishrant, many happy returns of the day to you, I'm wishing you a very happy birthday.

V: Thank you.

S: Thank you very much for showering your Buddha field on me. It gives me a lot of clarity and immense love, every time.

V: It's my love affair with humanity. I just love humans, but then again I love animals, I love plants and I love this: the most beautiful thing here is love, you know,

and all you've got to do is be wide open and the perception of love is always here. It's only in closure that we miss love. So I love what I do, I love you, the world.
S: The sleepiness that I feel because of lack of sleep, and because of the grinding of my head, namely mind, are they both equally intense energies?
V: Okay, so what I found with the sleepiness through lack of sleep, that doesn't usually destroy your clarity. What destroys your clarity is the tamasic energy that we produce when we overthink or when we worry or procrastinate, or if we pick it up if someone else is like that. So if you're feeling really drowsy, if you're feeling like you can't see clearly, it's probably energetic rather than tiredness.
S: Thanks Vishrant.
V: Thanks Abayhi.

~

S: The next question is as follows: Why is it important to clear my energy? Can I just be detached and observe it?
V: Yeah, you can, but even if you are detached and you're observing it, it's going to affect the way you feel and it's going to affect the way you think and it's going to affect others as well. The gift that we give everyone we meet is the energy we carry. I became very aware of this in my younger years because I was involved in helping people become successful, and it's pretty hard to help people become successful if you're carrying a dense energy that clouds them out. And as I went further on in life, I started to recognise that as a naturopath and psychotherapist, my job was

to lift people, not sink them with the density I may have produced or the density that I was carrying from other people. I saw there was a fault in that. My job was really to try to lift people – including my wife, my kids, my friends, whoever I met – because whatever energy we carry, is our gift to everyone we meet.

S: The following question has been written by a viewer: I have been serious since I was born and when I practise being present, I get even more serious. How can I be non-serious?

V: Come and see me and we'll tickle you until you stop being serious. Seriousness is just fear-based, so allow the worst to occur. Be okay with everything and fear will drop. Surrender. Accept life as it is. Seriousness is you trying to manipulate and control a result. Let go, let go, let go. Be in flow. And by the way, there's no way you're serious when you were born. That's not possible. Something frightened you and you got serious. Let go, let go, let go. Be free.

I was thinking we could tickle that person but I don't know where they are.

Hi Susha.

S: I thought that was brilliant. Getting tickled. Oh, happy birthday Vishrant.

V: Thank you Susha.

S: I want to ask you about, is it possible for energies to just go through us and not get stuck in us? I think you have said something about the belief systems. Can you elaborate a little more? How and why am I holding them and getting sick sometimes? What can I do so they just go through me?

V: Yeah, so I absorb everything that comes anywhere near me, but it doesn't get stuck, and I had to have a look at this for why is it so? Why does it not get stuck? Why does it not stick in me? I started looking at babies, and I've had three of them, and they're pristine. They're absolutely pristine. They can take on enormous amounts of energy from adults around them and within moments be energetically clean again. I realised the difference between a baby and an adult is the mind. The mind has the potential to harbour density because of its belief systems, so I got the understanding that the reason people harbour certain types of energy is because they have pain bodies and the belief systems they have that support these pain bodies harbour energy.

As you undo your belief systems, as you undo your mind, you become less likely to harbour density that you pick up from others. So the whole idea of higher consciousness and spirituality is a stripping-down process. It's not a building-up process. It's an undoing process, so as you undo your mind – as you undo the belief systems that you've had programmed into you by your parents, society, religion, whatever else – you become less likely to hold energy of any kind. So energy comes in, it stays a while, and then it gets expanded out now. Earlier years I took on so much working as a psychotherapist because people were in misery. They don't come to see psychotherapists unless there's something's wrong so before I'd go and be with my family, cuddle my kids, give my wife a hug, I'd clear my energy. I'd jump under a cold shower until the energy dissipated or I'd dance and I found after some particularly heavy sessions, I'd be dancing for an hour, but I used to love dancing so that was cool, and then I'd go and hug my kids and hug my wife because I didn't want to pass the energy that I picked up from my client base to my kids or my wife. I saw that as a disservice to them.

S: So would you say that all of the belief systems, all beliefs need to go before one can be in that place with that? That would be awakening?

V: Yeah, that's a great idea. I like that. I see all beliefs, all belief systems as prisons, all of them, and people die to protect their prisons, die to protect their beliefs, and they're all prisons. We don't need a heap of beliefs to live in the world. I've got a "maybe" with just about everything. It's nice. I don't get caught in anything as a result. People have the belief system that people shouldn't betray them. I don't have that belief system. That would be me being out of touch with reality because people do betray, but most people don't examine their belief systems, they just believe them to be true. That of course gets caught every time. The belief system is somehow challenged. Every time they're challenged, they contract, they go into suffering because they resist life. Not a nice way to live. Undo all of your belief systems. Be free. Be free, be free, be free. All belief systems are prisons. Undo them.

S: So when I tried to undo them I guess I don't know how to know I have undone them enough. I'm still getting caught once in a while with something. I can let go sooner. I used to brood for two days. Now it's maybe half an hour, maybe less.

V: You're getting better then. You see, all belief systems have support beliefs as well. They have defence systems supporting them. Those defence systems also have to be taken down. Support systems are justifications. For example, the belief that I shouldn't be betrayed by someone has support systems. "That's wrong, they shouldn't be like that, I'm not like that so they shouldn't be". These are all justifications for supporting the belief that you shouldn't be betrayed. Now those support beliefs or justifications also need to be undone.

S: Okay, I need to see them all.

V: Up to you. We were so free when we were born and we're so free up till about three years of age and then we start developing our minds. We went to school and we learned how to live in our heads. And my goodness, most people never recovered.

S: That's true. Thank you so much.

V: Thank you, Susha.

~

S: Next question has been written by Abigail: Whenever I'm riding my bicycle, I experience brief moments of no thought, but when the mind comes back again, it feels noisier. How do I come back to no thought?

V: Okay, the reason it seems noisier is because you haven't been thinking and you've just noticed the noise. It's probably been just as noisy the whole time before, but because it was continuous, you weren't noticing how noisy it was. When it came back after the brief period that you had no-mind, it just seemed very noisy. You want to actually move more into no-mind, find something that brings you into the present moment, find something that grips you so firmly in the moment that you can't move out of it. For me, that was riding motorbikes and rallying cars and diving underwater in dangerous territory, and martial arts, sport, rugby, gymnastics. I had a lot of different things I did that brought me firmly into the moment. When I was at school, I played handball. If you're not present, you lose. It's very simple. When we went into class, we developed a pattern of living in our heads, thinking and problem solving. Unfortunately, it became a default pattern and now you're stuck in it. Meditation or the practice of meditation – which is the practice of putting your awareness on something that is real – helps change that pattern back to how you were when you were a little kid, when you were about two, because little kids are very present. They haven't learned to live in their heads yet. Meditation helps you reclaim reality from the dream that you're lost in. Anything that brings you to the moment is worthy. Anything. But don't think about it, do it.

I found that when I started practising formal meditation, which for me was watching the breath at my lip, it was easy. I didn't know why it was so easy for me until I had a look at how I lived my life. I was very much into the present moment. I liked things that kept me present. I liked going fast on my motorbike. I liked rallying cars, I liked playing rugby, I liked martial arts, I liked gymnastics, I liked dancing. I liked anything that brought me back into the moment because it's so free in the moment. There's no freedom living in your mind. It's a prison full of belief systems. Anything you can do to bring you back to the moment is worthy. When I decided to walk around Australia after being a businessman – I did four years of that – I'd noticed that I was a little stuck in my head, so I took my shoes off and I walked around Australia for four years barefoot. That might sound really odd, but that's what I did because I wanted to feel the earth under my feet. I wanted to get back to reality. I didn't want to live in my head. Reality is quite beautiful. I don't think anyone's head is beautiful. We just problem solve because that's what we learned to do at school. So I walked around Australia with bare feet and if I could walk on a railway line I would, barefoot, because you cannot be anything other than present to reality when you're walking barefoot on a railway line. I loved walking for kilometres and kilometres and kilometres on railway lines – just to be so present, to develop that pattern of being present to reality because I love it. I love the present moment. It's up to you. What do you practise? Because whatever you practise, you're going to be good at, and if all you practise is thinking, dreaming, that's all you're going to be good at. That's how it is.

S: The next question is from Tyler.

V: Hi Tyler.

S: My question was: do you recall a specific moment where you went from being asleep, to waking up or knowing yourself? Are you able to recall a specific moment where that happened?

V: It's not that clear because before awakening I had had a year of satoris, a year of glimpses of true self, and before awakening I'd been in retreat with an awake teacher for two weeks. During that two weeks, I was floating on the coat tails of the teacher. I was finding Beingness as self because of the energy of the teacher. Then the teacher went away and I went back to Perth, back home, and I found that it was still there. There was just no Vishrant. There was just vast, vast nothingness as self. I woke up the day after retreat and it was still there and my mind was surprised because it didn't expect that, just this wide space and an absence of the "I". And I think every day for the next week that I woke up, there was that surprise from the mind's perspective. "Ooh, it's still here, wooh" – and it's been like that now for 22 years.

So it wasn't a specific thing, because there was a whole year of satoris. Thousands of satoris because I was self-inquiring for that year, asking the question, "What's aware?" And that question, what's aware, would take me into satori. But the satoris wouldn't last. Awareness would come back to the mind and would leave itself and I'd find myself ego-based again. So there was no specific time that it occurred. When awakening was final, it was in the presence of an awake teacher that Beingness was aware of itself and that stayed, but during that year of satoris, the mind recognised clearly that what was required on its part was surrender, so everything that was presented was surrendered, everything, until there was nothing in the way anymore. There was just let go, let go, let go. Anything that contracted? Everything was surrendered. Everything was given to God. Nothing was held on to. Nothing. Anything that you hang on to brings you back to the ego. It's a prison. Attachment is a prison.

S: Thanks for answering the question.

V: Okay, Tyler.

~

S: The next question has been written by a viewer: Is forcefully breathing out clearing?

V: Heck no. Might be clearing your nose. This game is not about forcing anything. This game is about relaxing, about being cool. It's not about forcing anything. It's not about being yang, it's about being yin. Let-go is not yang, it's yin. Acceptance is not yang, it's yin. The pathway to higher consciousness is let-go. Acceptance, openness – nothing to do with force of any kind.

S: The next question has been written by Shyena: Is burning plants such as sage effective for clearing?

V: Not in my experience, Shyena. I know of the practice, I just can't see how it can possibly work. Energy is energy. I don't think it's affected by smoke or perfume. Everything is energy, even the smoke is energy, but I don't think it has the ability to clear density and people or rooms or anything like that. You want a room cleared? You get someone who's really clean to clear for you. It's very simple. Energy flows from full to empty. You want to clear a room? Open the doors, open the windows, let whatever's inside out. You want to clear yourself? Stop thinking, get present to reality. Go jump in a river or the ocean or under a shower. Have a good dance. That works.

S: The next question is from a viewer: When lifting people, how much of it do you attribute to energy and how much to words and action?

V: You can inspire people with words. You can inspire people with action. It's true. Being able to lift people energetically is a whole other game. It means you have to be emptier than everybody else. As you take on their density, they get lighter and they get lifted. That's a job and a half in itself because you have to be empty. You can have all of the inspirational words in the world and be full as a goog with density, tamasic and rajasic energy. You're not going to lift people too high. People who can really lift people are actually empty.

Some people asked me about shamanism. The shaman is empty. If the shaman's not empty, the shaman is not a shaman. The shaman lives in the energy world. The shaman's empty. So, the shaman can take density out of other humans and help heal them. This is how shamanism works. It's in the energy world. It's all in the energy world. So the shaman and the mystic both live in the energy world. The energy world is real, but a lot of people don't perceive it because they're too locked in their minds. Energy is everything. Everyone's putting out energy constantly. It can be read, but not if you're living in your head. You have to become quiet inside and you have to become relatively empty inside yourself to perceive the energies that are around you. The shaman and the mystic can play with energy because they live in the energy world. They don't live in their heads.

S: The next question has been written by Christopher: Are energy fields always easily distinguished between positive and negative?

V: Positive and negative is the wrong way to look at it. Is the energy negatively affecting you in a way that makes you feel cloudy? Or is it allowing you to see? Is it giving you a clarity? See, the lack of energy gives us clarity, but human beings produce a whole pile of different types of energy depending on what they're thinking. You want clarity? You have to stay pristine. I wouldn't see it as negative or positive. It's just what it is, but if you're really interested in higher consciousness, you need clarity. You can't have clarity if you're full of dense, painful energy or dense active energy. You have to become clear and then you can see clearly. That's up to you. You're the one who produces or you're the one who contains. What in your life do you do to stay pristine? In Hinduism, they have the three goonas: tamasic, rajasic and sattvic. The whole idea is to go to sattvic. I agree. Sattvic is brilliant. Being pristine is brilliant. You see everything. It's like sitting on top of a mountain. You can see everything. If you follow rajas – which is active energy, anxious energy, irritated energy – you don't see much. If you're full of tamasic energy, which is that sleepy, tired, unconscious type of energy, well you don't see much. Energy and the understanding of energy in spirituality or higher consciousness is actually essential. Clarity rules.

S: The next question has been written by Santosh. Namaste, I'm having some issues with my daily meditation practice. I've been practising breath-watching meditation since December. It was going well until September. Since then, I have had the urge to puke in the middle of meditation. I took a break for a few weeks and started meditation again, but still the same issue. Since last month, I have been dry retching every morning. The doctors couldn't find any issues. I also had spontaneous kundalini awakenings in April and May which also add pressure inside my head and forehead. Can you please comment?

V: Okay. Yeah, I'm glad you've been to see a doctor and ruled out anything medical, because it's important that you do that. If it's not medical, it's energetic, which means you're probably purging pain body, stuff that you've picked up in this lifetime and repressed – wounding, trauma, stuff you've carried from previous lifetimes – and it's coming out. People think, "Oh, I'm going to meditate and find peace". Highly unlikely, because we repress so much stuff, we hold so much in, and when we meditate, it relaxes the mind and all the coping mechanisms that are holding the pain bodies in, dissipate, and what's inside comes out and it can make you sick. If it's making you sick, it's probably repressed fear, anxiety, but it's energetic and you're energetically purging. You're physically vomiting, but you're energetically purging. This is a result of meditation, because meditation relaxes the mind and then everything that's being held down starts to come out and people don't expect this. They think, "Oh, I meditate, I should find peace". Yeah, in the beginning you will, but then you're going to purge everything you've been carrying. Anything that you've repressed is going to start coming out because the body is holding it in, it's being held prisoner. So you be okay with the purging. You make it okay. If it's not medical, you just make it okay and you keep going because it's just old stuff leaving, old energy leaving, and this is good, not bad. So don't stop. Keep going.

~

S: So this topic has been really important to me because I feel like this is a big obstacle that I've been going through with this energy thing. My question to you is: I saw you answer about cold water and you shower with cold water. Now I like to shower with hot water.

V: Look, I used to shower with hot water as well, and then at the end I'd turn the cold on full and the hot off full and it would shock any energy I was carrying out of my body. It's the shock that takes it out. It only takes surface energy out, but it takes some out. It shocks it out.

S: Okay. I also recently bought a trampoline, like a mini trampoline. I find that is helping me.

V: Absolutely, yep. I used to have those too. I used to like to dance on it. I used to put music on and dance on the trampoline.

S: That sounds good. For me, my ultimate passion since childhood that I've had is sports, and because I'm in Canada and it's snowing here and sports require, like, different kinds of things around it, like you need the right kind of people and the equipment or the field, so not to be able to do something that I love the most, which is to play sport, is also not very fun for me.

V: So whereabouts actually are you and how cold is it?

S: It's in Ontario. So it's pretty, pretty cold right now. Like, minus eight I think right now.

V: Minus eight, that's not that cold.

S: It's not that cold right now so I do go for a run. I enjoy running.

V: You could go for runs in that, but you might need to be dressed. I spent some time in Canada as well, and in Oregon, and it gets pretty cold there in the winter, 20 below.

S: Right. I found that walking, walking in the cold you know, was pretty good.

V: Yeah. Because the cold takes it out of you. I don't recommend swimming.

S: It's funny how you said you walked barefoot in Australia. I do the same, not barefoot, but sometimes I go barefoot outside in my garden.

V: It allows you to feel the earth. It puts your awareness on what is real, because your feet and your feelings in your feet are real, so it's a meditation. It's a meditation practice.

S: Absolutely. And they also sometimes run and jog without the clothes.

V: Have you got snow there at the moment?
S: It melted today actually. So I think it's positive one or two. But yeah.
V: I used to like to play in the snow because that brings you very present as well.
S: Right, right.
V: Yeah. There are lots of different things you can do and make them fun, you know, because you don't have to be serious about any of this. I used to like to make angels in the snow by laying on my back and waving my legs back and forth and having a look at the angel I'd created in the snow.

See, as adults, we think we're not supposed to play and we're not supposed to be silly, but heck, why not? Why not play? Why not be silly? Why not have fun?
S: Yeah, this reminds me of working in long-term care and I see a lot of seriousness in the old-age home. There's one person, his name is Dino, he's Italian, and he's like a kid. And I see the difference, you know, with seriousness and just playfulness and I'm trying to get back to my playfulness because I feel like I've gotten a bit serious with working in the long-term care.
V: Yeah. Vasu, you'd love playing with me here, mate. When we go shopping, right, we go to Coles which is a supermarket, and in the supermarket they have music and they have bright lights and they have wide aisles and you can dance. You can dance to the music and you can actually swing the trolley around so it goes in circles and have a great deal of fun. There's no need for us to be so frightened of what people think of us. We don't play. This guy Dino, he's obviously not

scared of what people think of him and he's having a nice life as a result. He's playing. What a wonderful thing to do for yourself and for others, to play.

S: Yeah, absolutely. Sorry for taking the time guys and thank you Vishrant.

V: I'm here. I'm here for you, man and I hope that you play more.

~

S: The next question has been written by Prem Prabhat: There's a lot of mention about vibes or vibrations in the spiritual circles. What's been your experience with different vibes and how does it affect people?

V: Right. You know, the vibe I liked the best was the vibe I got from my awake teachers from the Buddha field – the vibe that expanded my mind, expanded my Heart, and took me into the nothingness. That was my true self. That's the best vibe of all, the Buddha field around someone who's awake. Such an amazing light. But all human beings create energy fields with the way they think and what they've picked up from others and what they carry and you could say they have vibes. Angry people have a vibe. Sad people have a vibe. Happy people have a vibe. Loving people have a vibe. Frightened people have a vibe. It's all vibes. Actually, if you're sensitive enough, you can feel it. Unfortunately, people can get very caught in that world too. The best you can do for you is to become as clear as possible, become sattvic, becoming empty. And now you're headed towards higher consciousness. This is the best, but it's up to you. You're going to create your reality by the way you think.

S: Next question has been written by Milan: How can I support my kids who are teenagers and overwhelmed with school and thinking, but also comparing themselves with other kids?

V: Okay, so I raised three children and you know the thing that is best for them is love, but also you need to have your boundaries in place because they are kids, they are not adults, they need to have boundaries for them, but they need to know they're loved. The greatest thing you can give your children is your love and always loving them. It's also one of the greatest things you can do for yourself because when you're loving, you're enjoying life. Loving is beautiful. Always be the loving back-up for your kids.

With my kids, I had boundaries for them though, you know, because they're kids. They don't really know what's right and wrong. They don't know what's so good for them. They need your adult understanding of the world. They need your boundaries, but as long as there's love with it, as long as you're on their side as well. Children who are raised in love do very well. It's up to you. How loving can you be? How caring can you be while still putting the boundaries that are required in place?

S: The next question is from Marcus: I've been getting good at accepting. I feel more at ease. You've said that acceptance comes first. What comes next?

V: Okay, so my teacher Osho or Bhagwan Shree Rajneesh taught witnessing the mind. Now if we witness the mind, we see an awful lot of things. Without judgement, we just see them. In witnessing what we see, if we start practising acceptance of ourselves as a human being, just as a psyche, forget about Beingness, the mind becomes whole. While the mind is not accepting itself totally, it is not whole. There's part of it that is judging another part and holding it in contempt. So the first two things: watching the mind, witnessing the mind and then accepting the mind as it is, and in that acceptance of the mind, you start to find out that it extends externally from you as well. The more you accept yourself as you are, the more you accept the world as it is, because you see that everything in the world is also inside of you. We begin with witnessing. We accept what we see, and in that acceptance, the mind relaxes. Now we've developed the mind that is ready for self-inquiry: a mind that is relaxed, a mind that is at ease. The foundation work has been done. The foundation work is self-acceptance.

S: The next question has also been written by Marcus: How can you turn any action into an energy-clearing practice?

V: By being aware of the action. People move their hands, but they're not aware they're moving their hands because they're too locked in their heads. When you move your hand, be with the movement. When you move your legs, be with the movement. When you move your head, be with the movement. Every action can be a meditation if you have awareness on it. When we're present to reality, we are clear. It's really only when we're present to our mind that we create density. Every action, we can be aware of it. Every movement, we can be aware of it, or we can dream while it happens by itself.

S: The next question has been written by Christopher: When you look at other humans, are you looking at energy fields rather than just bodies?

V: Before a person says hello to me, they've already been read energetically. Not because I try to read people, I just can't help it. I pick everything up because everyone is radiating. Everybody is radiating how they think and how they feel. Everybody is radiating the energy they carry, everybody, and I can't help but pick it up because I'm wide open. So it's not like I'm deliberately reading people, it just happens. It happens that I see people and I read, and their energy shows itself to me at the same time. Or I don't see people and they walk into the room behind me and I read them because energy shows itself. Everyone is radiating. Everyone is a radio station putting out whatever energy they're carrying and it can be read. It just happens.

S: Are there any beings that cannot be read?

V: I couldn't read Osho. I couldn't read Bhagwan Shree Rajneesh. I couldn't read him. All I could pick up was emptiness. It was like he wasn't there. But there was a field of energy that was kilometres wide. That was just beautiful, and that was the Buddha field that was produced by awareness aware of itself inside of him. But trying to read him was an impossibility. There was just nothing there. There was a nobody. I found the same with most of my other teachers. There was nothing there, just an emptiness.

Whereas people who are ego-based, there's always something there. There's always a contraction of some kind, a density of some kind. It's the ego. In Osho, there was an absence. I couldn't read him. He was the first person I'd ever met who I couldn't read. I got into the energy world when I was very young and I could read people by the time I was 20, quite clearly. To be in the energy world, I had to be pretty silent inside of my own mind because the noisier you are, the less you perceive energetically. To really perceive energy well, you need to be quiet inside. So I was measuring people for a long, long time. I think I was 28 when I met Osho or something like that, or 30, and I just I couldn't believe it. He was the first person I ever came across who I couldn't read. There was just nothing there. And it made me realise there were different types of people on the planet. This man was awake and he wasn't living as an ego. He wasn't living a "normal" life. He was living the life of someone who was awake. He was living as Beingness rather than living as an "I". It really inspired me to have a closer look, to go for it, to go for higher consciousness, to go for Heart, to go for Enlightenment. He was a great inspiration.

~

S: Um, so I read something from Osho recently. He talked about doctors and people in the medical industry having to have something which can make them toughen up because they work in areas where there's a lot of sadness and problems and if they see that on a regular basis, they have to fully toughen up. Could you explain what he means by toughen up? Is that because of the energy? I'm making no sense. Are they defending their energy, having a rebellious energy, to protect themselves? Could you explain?

V: I'm not sure in what context Osho was talking, but people on the frontline, the medical frontline, have to be able to deal with things that can quite often be very shocking. Car accidents, all sorts of different tragedies, people dying, people being burnt, all sorts of different things they need to be involved in and they can harden up and defend themselves against it or they can open up and accept it as it is. In the opening, it can be dealt with. In the acceptance of it as it is, it can be dealt with, but it can also be dealt with by becoming hard and calloused as well. Now in spirituality, that's the wrong direction. In spirituality, if we're going for higher consciousness, we don't defend ourselves. We open up completely and go the other way, open up and accept life exactly as it is. And in that acceptance, we can deal with anything. It's only in resistance to what is that we have problems. That's where suffering begins, in resistance. Walking through the world, open and vulnerable is the way of the sage, is the way of the mystic, is the path of the disciple. All defences are in the way. All protective devices are in the way. All closures are in the way. Openness counts for everything.

S: Thank you, Vishrant.

V: Thank you. And thank you for satsang. Good to see you bravehearts here today.

CHAPTER TEN

What Are the Obstacles to Happiness?

V: Welcome to satsang.
S: Hello Vishrant, can you please talk about what are the obstacles to happiness?
V: The problem lies in our programming really. None of us were programmed to be happy. I can't recall being programmed to be happy at school and I cannot recall my parents programming me to be happy either. As a matter of fact, from memory, I was programmed to be an efficient little machine for 12 years at school. We're not actually programmed to be happy, but what we are programmed to do is to solve problems. We spend all of this time at school learning how to solve problems, learning how to repeat answers so we can get a mark, so we can get a diploma or a degree, but that doesn't make us happy. What it does is it sets us up for a life of solving problems, and living in your head solving problems is not happiness.

Then we go a little bit further and see that we desire things, and we constantly desire things. We want things to be different than how they are and in this very desiring, we are discontent, and you can't call discontentment happiness. Also, we achieve things, we get things, we own things, and then we get fearful of losing those things. So our attachment to the things that we have – whether it's our relationships or whether it's material objects – create suffering for us also because we resist losing them. We go into resistance and resistance equals suffering. We were never, ever programmed to be happy. We were actually programmed to be unhappy, to constantly desire what we haven't got. We look at ambition and in the West, ambition is seen as a wonderful thing. I know for a fact that someone who's ambitious is more dissatisfied with life than anyone else. I don't see that as a merited thing. I don't see that as a good thing. I see that as detrimental. I mean, don't we go for quality of life? Don't we go for happiness? Yet in our society we're not programmed for it. We're actually programmed to be discontent through our desires, through our attachments, through our constant problem solving, our living in our heads. Where in society do they teach you how to be happy?

Well, the answer to that of course is satsang. It's one of the reasons I was so interested in higher consciousness because it is about happiness. If we serve Heart we can be manageably happy. If we find ourselves as Beingness, then there is profound contentment for no reason which is my definition of happiness. Most people pretend to be happy. You ask them, "How are you?" and they'll say "I'm good". Really? Are you? While you're continually desiring things to be different than how they are or to get things you haven't got? While you're terrified of losing what you have? You're telling me you're happy? I don't think so. I think you need to get honest with yourself and have a look. Everyone's pretending to be happy because when you say you're happy, people accept you. It's one of the ways we get acceptance. But are you really happy? Are you really, really happy? Or are you actually running a lot of discontent because you want things to be different than how they are while pretending to be happy?

This is one of the things that you get to see when you start witnessing your own mind instead of believing it. When you start witnessing it, you watch what it does. You watch how it behaves. I think all human beings want to be happy. I think all human beings would like to have a lifestyle that they enjoy, but where do we actually get programmed for that to occur? We definitely get programmed to make more money so we can develop a lifestyle that might be better than other people's lifestyles, but does that make us happy? Probably not. Probably not at all because we're still stuck with a mind that's constantly desiring things to be different than how they are. We're still stuck with a mind that is going to get fearful of losing what it has. The only way that I know to get free is to go beyond the mind. That's Enlightenment. Up to you. This is your life. Whatever you practise, you're gonna get good at.

Are there any questions, any statements, any challenges to this teaching today?

S: The first question: Do you think spiritual seekers are more likely to be happy?

V: Heck no. No, they want to get free. It's another desire, isn't it? They want to get free. They want to raise the consciousness levels. More desires. The more effort you put into any desire, the more dissatisfied you actually are, the more unhappy you are. The only thing that really works with higher consciousness is a level of totality, so on the way there's a fair bit of unhappiness. What I found in the seeking of higher consciousness was that in service of Heart, we can find what I call manageable happiness because when I was helping people in whatever way I was helping them, it made me feel good. I felt good to be helping people. But it was conditional on me helping people. When awareness became aware of itself, there was profound contentment for no reason at all. That's different. It wasn't conditional. Awareness was aware of itself and there was profound contentment. In other words, happiness.

~

S: Vishrant, good morning. Thank you. I'm not sure how to phrase this as a question. So I'll make a statement and perhaps you can help me to unravel it. Yes, a lot of what you've said resonates with me because I tend to want to be honest with people when they ask me how I am. And when I tell them, "Hmm, I'm not sure, today I'm feeling rather discontent," they're not sure how to respond to that. It makes it a bit difficult to have normal social engagement sometimes. I guess I just wanted to say that yes, it's my experience too, discontent and resistance seem to have been common themes. And the resistance in particular from my recent learnings is something I'm finding very difficult to take care of. And perhaps you can tell us a little bit more about overcoming resistance and discontentment, if you're able to, please?

V: Well, I have a problem sharing my condition with people too because people ask me how I am and I have two answers. One is, I'm always the same because I am, and the other is, I'm lovely, because that's how I feel, and people have trouble handling that. What I learned – and I learned this a long time ago – is that acceptance takes away most of our suffering because acceptance is non-resistance. When we are in resistance, we're usually in non-acceptance of what is in some way. Acceptance is something we were never taught to practise, but it can give us quite a nice life if we accept things as they are, rather than our preferences. I started practising acceptance 40 years ago, because it works. As a matter of fact, if you accept something, there's no story anymore, it's over. That's the indication that the acceptance has been total, but I wasn't taught that at school either, or by my parents. That was something I picked up from Eastern teachers, Osho Rajneesh and a few others. This is what they teach because acceptance leads us to be able to surrender unconditionally. The more resistance we put into anything – in other words, the more non-acceptance we put into anything – the more we suffer, but we're doing it to ourselves. It's not like someone else is doing it to us, Steven, we do it to ourselves. That's a big realisation in itself: that it's not the world that hurts us, it's us that hurts us with the way we think about the world with our reactions to the world. That realisation isn't enough to change us. We have to change our patterning because we've all been patterned to resist. We're a warrior breed. We resist, resist, resist, suffer, suffer, suffer, and then share our suffering with the people we love. But we can program ourselves to start accepting life instead of resisting life through repetition. Not through understanding, because understanding doesn't work. Through repetition: practising acceptance instead of practising resistance.

I wish there was an easy way. I wish there was, but there's not. Practice is the only way that we can change the default patterns of our mind.
S: Thank you. Thank you. Yes, appreciate that.
V: Steven, do me a big favour and practise some acceptance and see.

As of right now. Right now.
S: Very good. Thank you.
V: Thank you, Steven. Hello Susha.
S: Vishrant, you said that those of us who have glimpses of the Truth feel more dissatisfied. And I do, and I agree to that, and especially when the ego-based reality hits, it's like going from heaven to hell, or going from the sky to the underworld or something like that.
V: That'll do.
S: I wonder if manageable happiness is what one should look for in that time. What is the path? When you had satoris and you were not awake, then you went for manageable happiness, that wasn't really happiness, right? You were still yearning for something else?

V: No, it was happiness. I got a great deal of joy out of being in service to other human beings. I went back to school and trained as a naturopath and psychotherapist so I could have tools to help other people with, and I found that when I was helping people, I was happy. I spent the 10 years or 11 years before awakening helping people because I loved it. I loved helping people. It just made me feel good. I wasn't doing it to make myself feel good. That was just a byproduct of being in service to humans and plants and animals and whatever else I could find. I'd lived 33 years or 34 years of my life as a selfish human being, being very successful at that, but it was so hollow, it was so empty, it was so loveless. When I started moving and opening my Heart, moving towards service, it all changed. From my perspective, I didn't start living until I was 34. That's when my Heart started opening and that's when I started being in service of other human beings. That was wonderful, and at 45, I woke up.

S: So what does a seeker do with this dissatisfaction that you talked about?

V: From my perspective, the totality that's required to change patterns in itself causes dissatisfaction, but it's worthwhile. If we don't change the patterns of our mind, they just run rampant, they just run the same. So from being a selfish human being just serving myself, I changed to a human being who served others, and I loved it. I loved helping people. It made my whole life richer and better and happier. Of course, there was still the dissatisfaction somewhere that I wasn't awake because I'd had satoris and I knew what awake was. And of course, there were the other patterns that came in, the other desires that came in, but because I was conscious enough, I could see them and I wasn't giving them much credence.

I was just talking to Steven about acceptance. Well, I practised acceptance. I accepted life as it was. I accepted what I had. I accepted what I got. When things went bad, I accepted that. When they went well, I accepted that with the same amount of passion. Acceptance is the key. It teaches us unconditional surrender, which prepares us for Enlightenment.

S: So are you saying whatever you're dissatisfied with, accept it?

V: I am saying that. Yes. I don't see the mind as the enemy. It's not the enemy. It's just doing what it does. It just can be reprogrammed. You don't have to fight it. You just have to reprogram some of the things in it that are in the way of being successful at higher consciousness and being successful at happiness. Any belief system that creates misery in you through victim-orientated thinking is in the way. It's worth challenging. It's worth putting doubt into.

S: Yes, and there are some that don't even show up. Like, they're not visible as belief systems and I'm never sure what it is and where the resistance comes from. At least I have a hard time. Sometimes I can't see them until much later.

V: Yeah, you've got to keep watching. For a lot of years, I used the outward breath to let go, you know? I'd find myself a little uptight and I'd just allow myself to die on the outward breath. And in that I got to see the things that were creating the tension in me, creating the contractions and the resistance, but it was a slow process. I do not think higher consciousness for anyone is a quick process. A lot of people make the huge mistake of collecting knowledge and thinking somehow that raises your consciousness levels. It not only doesn't raise your consciousness levels, it doesn't heal any wounds of your Heart, either. It's a booby prize. What works is practising something different than what you've done before. That's what works.

S: Thank you so much.

V: Thank you, Susha.

~

S: The next question has been written by a viewer: Acceptance leads to surrender, but where to draw the line of acceptance so that you don't end up being a doormat?

V: Okay, and so, you're being obnoxious? I accept that you're being obnoxious. Totally. And I walk away. How's that? And that walking away is not from a place of closure or a place of defensiveness. It's just what I do. And I do it from a place of accepting you as you are and accepting me as I am. People think that if we move to acceptance, we become impotent. I don't agree. We can do everything from acceptance. Acceptance equals openness. And openness is so cool.

I can accept everything and still say no from a place of acceptance. Try it and see. You'll know if you're actually doing it correctly, if you're wide open while you're doing it.

~

V: Hi Abhayi.

S: Hi Vishrant. Vishrant, in your satsang, I feel happy, there is happiness, there is self-acceptance, and even acceptance towards people or my situation in life, but it starts fading after satsang. So how can I be with you even after satsang?

V: Traditionally, satsang is held in the morning and in the evening, seven days a week. So 14 times a week, people who are seekers can come and rest in the energy field and use the clarity of satsang to see through their minds and remove obstacles and also ultimately use the Buddha field or the energy field of satsang to wake up. From my perspective, it is the freeway or the fastest way to be, in satsang. But as you go away from it, you go back to your mind, you go back to the way you were before. Try remembering what's been taught. See, Osho taught meditation, he taught watching the mind and he taught self-inquiry. This is what I practised. He taught openness. This is what I practised, and for me, I made it a game. If I found myself closed, the game was how fast can I open? If I found myself not present to reality, stuck in my head, how fast can I get back to reality? I made the whole higher consciousness endeavour a game, including self-inquiry. I just self-inquired to see what I'd find and I just kept doing it until I found Being-ness. A game. So meditation was a game. Self-inquiry was a game. Openness was a game. I called that game "the game of zero": Zero being when I'm absolutely at peace, and anything above that, not at peace. So if I found myself above, how fast can I get back to peace? How fast could I go down back to zero again? And I called this the game of zero. And I played it for 10 years. I loved it because people come along. They do things that upset you because of your belief systems that they shouldn't do those things. How fast can you get back to zero after you've been upset? And can you undo the belief systems that supported the contraction and resistance in the first place? It's just a game. Doesn't have to be hard work.

S: Yes, that makes a lot of sense, because I generally get caught up there and I take a long, long time to come back to the reality. But I think, like you said, if I make it a game, the approach is very different and even acceptance can come in.

V: Yeah, and you'll fail. We all fail. That's how we learn. We don't really learn as much from our successes as we do from our failures. That's how we learned to walk: by falling over and getting up again. And it's okay to fail. Just never give up. Treat it as a game that you like playing.

S: Yes.

V: I played the game of openness for a long time. It's a beautiful game because it ends with you being wide open.

S: Yes, I will do that. Thank you very much, Vishrant.

V: Thank you, Abhayi.

~

S: The following question has been written by Sita: Hi Vishrant, why is it you love dogs so much?

V: It's easy. It's easier to love dogs than it is to love human beings. Actually, I'll put that a different way:

it's easier to like dogs than it is to like human beings. I can't help but love human beings. I love everyone I meet – the good, the bad and the ugly – but it's easier to like dogs because dogs are so friendly. They're so forgiving. They just want to be your friend. They're wonderful. They're open. They say hello. Human beings are not so friendly. So I love dogs and dogs love you back. They can be your best friend. Yeah, I love dogs and I love humans. I love cats and I love birds and I love plants and I love trees and I love the rocks. I love the sky. I love. There's some things that I don't like. That doesn't mean I don't love them. I just don't like them. Certain behaviours, particularly human behaviours. There are some that are pretty abhorrent, but that's what is. I accept it. I don't like it, but I love the person.

S: Next, Sarah has a question.

V: Hello Sarah.

S: Good morning Vishrant. I'm experiencing a lot of fear around being fully seen and being vulnerable, and with that, somewhat of an intensification of self-sabotage.

V: Yeah. In what way? How are you self-sabotaging, Sarah?

S: I'm slipping into selfish thoughts about what I want which ultimately is more of a blanket protection to avoid really looking deep within myself and exposing everything.

V: Yeah, look, I've been at the game for a long time. I started when I was 19. This exposing yourself, you don't have to. All you've got to do is surrender. You don't have to really publicly expose yourself. You can surrender, but that takes a fair bit of practice too. I surrendered to God. I gave my life to God or Truth, whatever you want to call it. I don't think anyone knew but me. You know, there was no exposure to other humans. I just gave myself, my totality to God or Truth, and in that my whole life changed. I'd seen enough of what it was like to live selfishly and the rewards aren't that pleasant. I actually didn't think it was worth living any other way except in service, but that was probably because I'd been around the block a lot of times. I'd been beaten up by existence a lot of times. I'd had a lot of tragedy in my life. I could see that life was suffering. We lose everything, you know. We lose everything. It's just how it is. And for me, I didn't want to be selfish anymore. I wanted to find my Heart, and in finding my Heart, I wanted to be in service to everything besides me. Whether it was the Earth or the trees or the plants or the animals, the birds, the fish, human beings, it didn't make much difference. It was a way of life. The Way of the Heart is a way of life. It's a way of taking care, and if we really, really look at what it means to be a man or a woman who's mature, we're caretakers here. We are here to take care, and this is a mature role.

Unfortunately, we haven't all been taught that. I definitely wasn't taught that. I had to come to that through meditation. The situation I grew up in was attending a very competitive school where I was taught to be ambitious. And I was ambitious. And I was successful. I managed to beat a lot of people.

How ugly is that? That's what I was taught. It took me a long time to realise how ugly that was. That selfishness is not pretty. That it is not the Way of the Heart. It is the opposite.

So this fear of exposure? Nobody cares anyway. Everyone's thinking about themselves, you know? I like to think, and I have for a long, long time, that I'm God's fool and it's okay. Whatever people think of me, that's their problem, not mine. Life is a play, and we can play and play and play. The moment you move into the present moment, you start playing because you've moved out of the dream and into reality, and it's only in the dream that you're worried about what other people think of you anyway. In reality, we just play. Osho talked about Zorba the Buddha. Well, being in the moment, being in the moment, being in the present moment with reality, that's Zorba, and awareness knowing itself, that's the Buddha. And they're both worthy. They're both worthy to go for as human beings, both Zorba and the Buddha. They're good pursuits. You can't afford to serve fear, it'll keep you crippled. You've got to be brave, Sarah. Brave.

S: It's coming at the ego. Every time I feel like that, I feel myself rising. It's like the ego censors it and comes in with some kind of vengeance, and recently, I haven't been very good at bringing myself back. It's quite strong.

V: Well, your ego and your mind are just a survival mechanism, that's all they are really. You take away the personal and they're just a survival mechanism, but because of your intelligence, you can learn acceptance and surrender. You can learn to be free. But really, when you look at the mind, that's all it is. It's just trying to survive.

S: When you decided to give yourself to God, did you feel there was an intensification of ego?

V: No. For me, when I decided to give myself to God, it was like a death. It was like the thing that wanted to be someone died. It was a dropping. There was a big dropping. And instead of a big somebody here, it was diminished. It was like I found humility, and it was beautiful. Humility is an absence of the "I" basically, and it was beautiful. Then I walked through the world still ego-based, but basically as a no one going nowhere, because that's what we all are. We have this idea that we're somebodies. We have this idea that there's somewhere to go. There's nowhere to go. We're already here. And as far as being a somebody, well, that's just made up. We're really just nobodies going nowhere and what other people think of you, well, that's their business. Don't worry about what other people think. They're all crazy anyway. If you've watched your own mind for long enough, you realise that everybody's crazy. Everybody who's ego-based is pretending to be something they're not to start with.

S: It seems easy to forget that at times.

V: As soon as we go into any form of dream, we forget. We forget everything. And so projections forward like worry, procrastination, these are just dreams. Remembering the past is another dream. As soon as we go into the dream, we're lost. That's why it's really important to try to stay as present to reality as you can.

So how present can you stay for how long, I wonder?

S: I have one other quick question. Sometimes in stillness, in meditation, I feel an energetic pull with my head. More times than not it pulls to the right, occasionally to the left. I'm just wondering what that was. It's quite strong to the point where my chin is almost parallel with my shoulder.

V: So my approach to that would be to accept it and just let it be. I gave up fighting. I gave up resisting. I gave up even understanding. I just accepted whatever was, and in that acceptance, I found profound peace. People don't accept because they think it makes them impotent. That's not true. I still managed to support two families. I still managed to run my naturopathy and my psychotherapy business. I still managed to help people. And I was practising acceptance. You can do it. It's up to you. It's just so foreign to us to practise acceptance. We practise righteousness and arrogance. That's what we're good at. All human beings are good at that while pretending not to be. When you start serving Heart, when you start looking for ways to help other human beings, to help animals, to help the planet, and you start doing it, it changes your whole life because now you're caring, and this is a beautiful way to live.

S: So drop the curious nature and...?

V: Curiosity has brought you to where you are. Curiosity is part of being a seeker. Wanting to know the meaning of it all. What's the meaning of life? Who am I really? This curiosity is a healthy curiosity and

without it, no one would wake up. I'm not saying you don't keep going for higher consciousness. I'm saying that you practise acceptance, because really, unconditional surrender which is gained through the practice of acceptance is the key to Enlightenment. Okay, Sarah?
S: Yes. Thank you.
V: Thank you Sarah.

~

S: The next question has been written by Deepesh: Is practising acceptance done through the mind or how does acceptance work correctly?
V: Yeah, acceptance is done through the mind. Absolutely. And so is non-acceptance. Our resistance is done through the mind as well. Without a mind, there would be no resistance. Without a mind, there'd be no acceptance. Mind you, acceptance doesn't really have much of a look. It's more of a non-doing, whereas resistance has a look because it's a doing. But it's all mind. You can support acceptance or you can support resistance. Your choice. If I was you, I wouldn't support resistance because resistance equals suffering.

~

V: My Kalimba, hello.
S: I had trouble getting out of bed this morning, but fortunately, when I was being lazy, the lawn mowing people came and they were doing the lawns around the place, so I got up, which I'm pleased about. A few things you've said today resonate with me and I wanted to make a couple of statements and ask a

question. First one is puppies. Oh, absolutely. I'm on the same page with you. When I go walking on the beach, I always go up to puppies. I ask the owners first, go up and have a little chat and a pat. Occasionally, like yesterday, there was one that for some reason was just yapping and unfriendly. And it was like, I hadn't done anything or not. The onus is on him. So he's a bit grumpy like that. But also, babies, you're probably the same. If I walk down the path and there's somebody coming towards me with a pram or a baby in their arms, I just go so gooey. It's so lovely. Do you share that with babies as well? I guess you would.

V: I don't do it so much with babies because people can take offence to being too personal with their babies, but I definitely do it with puppies. I say hello to all of the dogs I come across because I love dogs. I'm a little bit more cautious with babies because parents can get offended, though when they're not looking, quite often, I'll wave.

S: I've never experienced that. Nearly always the parents go "Oh, that's lovely". You know? And sometimes if a baby's crying, I'll go up and say hello, and the baby will turn around and soon it'll stop crying.

Talking about how you feel about doing things with things that you're given, I have been having a few more mood swings lately than normal with my bipolar, but I do Meals On Wheels deliveries a couple of days a week and no matter how I feel, at the beginning of the day, when I've finished my Meals On Wheels, I feel so much better because the people

are so happy to see you and have a little bit of interaction. It's just such a lovely thing to do. I get more out of it than I put into it, if you know what I mean?
V: I do, yeah. Good for you, Kalimba.
S: I play in the local bridge club and we've got a couple there we play a silly game with scratchies (lottery tickets). We do it in reverse. If we beat them, then we have to buy the scratchies. The other day I bought one and I looked at it. The first prize is worth three brand new Mercedes Benzes and I just had this weird panic attack. If I'd won them, I wouldn't be able to drive one. I feel so embarrassed going anywhere in a brand-new Mercedes. I thought "Oh God, I hope we don't get it," which we didn't fortunately, but please comment on that one? What's that about? I would not be able to go downtown driving a brand-new Mercedes Benz.
V: You're concerned about what other people think of you?
S: Well, most of the time, I'm really not, but I just feel so embarrassed about it.
V: Yeah, because you're concerned about what other people think of you. You'd need to have a look at well, what does it mean, in other people's minds, to see you driving a brand new, expensive vehicle? What does that mean? How does that affect the image you think you should have? Or they should have of you?
S: Yeah, I guess to some extent, I'm just like, I'm happy with what I have. I've got a little Hyundai hatchback which I think is a better 2015 model or something like that. I'm perfectly happy with that lovely little thing. The Little Yellow Peril, we call it.

V: But you know, in witnessing your mind, you might see something else going on there, and that's the thing. Witnessing the mind shows you all of these different things that you may or may not like, but if you have a problem driving around the streets in a brand-new Mercedes, I wonder what's really going on back there? So just out of curiosity, have a look and see. Yeah, by the way, if you win three Mercedes Benz, brand-new Mercedes Benz, latest model, I'll have all three.

S: You're welcome. One last time, a little statement I get a lot. When you talk to Abhayi, sometimes you pronounce it Abhayi and then sometimes you're cheeky, you call her Abby.

V: I do. I do. You're right. Before awakening, I had a sick sense of humour. And after awakening, sick sense of humour. Before awakening, chopping wood and carrying water; after awakening, funny sense of humour. What can I say? The thing is, you know, you wake up, you have no fear of anything. You have no interest in what people think of you. They think bad things about you? Good for them. They think good things about you? Good for them. Enlightenment is the ultimate freedom from everything. You just don't care because it just doesn't matter anymore. You can have three brand-new Rolls Royces or 93 as I think Osho had, and drive a different one every day, and it just doesn't matter because nothing matters.

S: Alright Vishrant, thank you so much.

V: Yeah, keep doing the Scratchies, mate. I'll be waiting for the phone call.

[SINGING] "Oh Lord, won't you buy me a Mercedes Benz, my friends all drive Porsches, I must make amends."

Nice talking to you, Kalimba.

S: Thank you, Vish.

S: The next question has been written by a viewer: When everything is accepted, and in this process, ultimately, no one is left. Is that why surrender is called a non-doing?

V: It's called a non-doing because it is a non-doing. Best example of that is, someone throws something at you and you don't move. You don't contract, you don't resist, nothing moves. Someone abuses you. You don't move. Nothing moves. You may respond, but nothing moves inside. This is surrender. It's a non-doing. We are programmed to constantly react. But we can teach ourselves surrender, which is non-doing, and that is how we develop an equanimous mind – a mind that will support Enlightenment through the practise of acceptance, through the practise of let-go. Of course, that's what you have to practise, and it's good to practise, it's fun to practise. People look at spiritual practices as arduous. I didn't ever do, they were fun. I practised let-go. I practised acceptance. I practised meditation. I practised self-inquiry. I practised openness. And they're all fun because they're all games. So many times, people practise the game of suffering. That's not one of the games I'd like to practise.

S: The next question is from Sai.

V: Well, I thought you would have asked me, Tosh, how do we practise not suffering? And I would have had to say to you: stop resisting, Tosh.

S: Yes, thank you.

S: Hello, Vishrant.

V: Isn't it odd, Sai, that Tosh doesn't ask me the right questions? I have to ask myself and answer them.

S: Oh, it'd be a lot easier if you just came up with the right question to start with. It's a good thing you accept everything as it is.

V: Oh, absolutely.

S: I was listening to you speak with Abby a little bit earlier in the webinar and you were talking about practising the game of zero.

V: Yeah.

S: And just noticing the contractions and letting them go ... noticing the contractions and letting them go ... and the thing that occurred to me is, sometimes I find I won't be triggered by anything in particular, but I'll notice a closure or discomfort inside of myself. I feel like I should get underneath that and it will be a more peaceful place. But I know you've also talked about avoidance of what is and avoiding wounding and things like that. I'm wondering if you see a difference between practising the game of zero when there's obvious things that get triggered inside of you? Did you even practise the game of zero when you noticed subtle things, even in a quiet space, in your own time?

V: I practised zero all of the time. It was a great game because I was fascinated by the game of zero. I was fascinated by how cool and calm I could become, even while under fire, if I just kept removing belief systems that caused contraction in me. I was just fascinated by the whole process. I was fascinated by the fact that I did not have to create suffering in myself through resistance. It fascinated me. It gave me a whole other view of the material world, of how all of these people who are suffering are creating it for themselves and there is no need to do so. We can learn to let go, we can learn to accept and we can walk through the world as nobodies rather than pretending to be somebodies.

S: Yeah, that I've seen to some degree. It's just not wanting to avoid, like wanting to know....

V: You've lost it Sai. Tosh?

S: The next question has been written by a viewer: Hello Vishrant, Osho said that we are hypnotised and believe in this false illusion of "I". Is de-hypnotising possible so that this false sense of self drops?

V: No, no, no, no. After the first major satoris, it was clear to me that the "I" wasn't real and that it was just a fabrication, but it was still there. It wasn't until awareness locked onto itself in Enlightenment that the "I" dropped and then there was a sense of nobody here, nobody talking, nobody doing anything. Up until then there was an understanding that there was nobody, but there was still somebody. The "I" is the identified part of the mind and it's a part of the survival mechanism. And it does drop upon Enlightenment, but you can diminish it through putting yourself aside through being in service to others. You can diminish it. There's no doubt about that. But it doesn't drop until awakening occurs, in my experience.

S: The next question is from Brian who's written an email to you: Hi, Vishrant, I'm a college student in the United States and I'd love to come meet you. Currently, I'm conflicted because I'm trying to just focus on raising my consciousness and dropping all of my belief systems. My parents really want me to focus on looking for a job in the business world because that's what people in society do. I'm having a hard time expressing that I'm not interested in blindly following what society does and staying in lower consciousness. My parents are extremely supportive and are just concerned that I won't have a job and won't be able to support myself. I acknowledge this, but I know my priority is dropping all of these belief systems that have been programmed in my mind over the past 21 years. Can you give me any advice on this topic?

V: Bryan, I love the way you think because unlike you, I continued on after school and became quite successful, retiring at the age of 28 because I was so ambitious, and I wasted at least 33 years of my life in the pursuit of success. You're lucky because you're a lot younger. Go for Truth. Go for higher consciousness. Existence will find a way to take care of you. Don't waste a moment. I got to the top of the heap. I got to the top in business. I got to retire with the yachts and the Rolls Royces, the penthouses. I gave it all away. It's not worth anything. Higher consciousness, Heart, that's worth something. Nothing else is. If you haven't got Heart, you're broke. That's what I realised at the age of 33. I was broke. I had heaps of money and I had heaps of properties, but I was broke because I didn't have any Heart. Go for Heart. Put Heart first, always. Put higher consciousness first, always. Do not hesitate. Do not wait. You may not have a later. We don't know. We project that we're going to have a later. We don't know. We have now. This is real. This is the only time that's real. Go for Truth. Go for Heart. I'm glad your parents are supporting you. That's awesome. You won't be able to meet me for a while because of COVID, it's how it is. But I'm online a lot. Nine times a week actually. You have a talk to Tosh. See what we can arrange, if you want to attend more satsangs.

Thank you for satsang. Good to see you bravehearts here today.

About Vishrant

Vishrant is a contemporary mystic who offers a pragmatic path to higher consciousness.

He made a fortune in publishing as a young man, retiring at the age of 28, and then as a world traveller and student of personal development later met controversial Indian guru and spiritual teacher Bhagwan "Osho" Shree Rajneesh who initiated him into the world of higher consciousness and enlightenment.

That encounter led to Vishrant tasting unconditional love during a terrifying shipwreck off the Western Australian coast and then glimpsing his own true nature. After these revelations, he gave his multi-million dollar company to the staff who had served him so diligently for a decade, and then set off around Australia barefoot for the next four years while searching for how to open his Heart once and forever.

After Osho's death in 1999, Vishrant committed himself to the Way of the Heart while working as a naturopath and psychotherapist, running men's encounter groups and later serving a crop of Advaita Vedanta teachers who started visiting Western Australia at the end of the 1990s. Vishrant woke up in 1999 in the presence of one of those teachers.

Since then, Vishrant has held satsang and retreats, and runs a Mystery School in the Perth hills which is also available online for those seeking to find their true nature.

Vishrant's teachings are pragmatic and free of belief systems and religious ideologies. He sees himself as a reality teacher rather than a spiritual teacher and says spirituality has become an overused word. His invitation is for people to investigate the Truth through their own direct experience.

To get involved, visit vishrant.org.

www.ingramcontent.com/pod-product-compliance
Lightning Source LLC
Chambersburg PA
CBHW060352080526
44583CB00012B/278